exquisite
MATCHES
THE PAIRING OF WINE AND FOOD

PHILIPPE FAURE-BRAC

The World's Best Sommelier

exquisite MATCHES

THE PAIRING OF WINE AND FOOD

IN COLLABORATION WITH
Anne Vantal

PHOTOGRAPHY
Jean-Charles Vaillant

STYLIST
Eric Trochon

TRANSLATED FROM THE FRENCH BY
Florence Brutton

EPA

MEAT

The pleasure you take in wine and food depends largely on your culture. There is the northern culture (Europe and North America) that prefers to drink wine on its own, outside meals. And there is the Mediterranean culture that nearly always associates wine with the pleasures of eating. I belong to the latter category. In the course of my 20 odd years as a sommelier, I have often had to taste wines on their own; but I have also spent a great deal of time exploring fine food and wine combinations. What began as a general interest soon became an all-consuming passion that opened up a wealth of unexpected pleasures. This book is the sum of those experiences.

Gastronomy, whether in France or elsewhere, is plainly in decline - people simply don't have the time for it anymore. But traditions live on, and there are still plenty of occasions for special meals, whether to entertain friends or celebrate a family get-together. The meal itself can be as uncomplicated as you like, but you do have to think carefully in advance – what dishes to serve and with what wines. Whatever your time and money constraints, you have a huge choice of options. One of the first lessons I ever learned as a 'wine and food matchmaker' is that there is in practice virtually no such thing as the best possible combination. In most cases, a number of permutations would be equally acceptable.

I have thought a lot about the origins of this complicity between certain wines and certain dishes. You can approach it from the perspective of what I call 'historical' associations. Or you can simply use creative thinking. Personally, I always try to keep an open mind, considering all of the options as impartially as I can. It would be wrong to think, for instance, that historical, geographical and regional alliances were purely a matter of tradition. In truth, products and wines from the same terroir have evolved side by side for so many years that it is hardly surprising they should go well together. Like an old married couple, they have the advantage of a life in each other's company. No surprise then that they should in time become perfectly compatible.

There are several factors to take into account when looking for more ambitious food and wine combinations. There is aroma – which relates directly to taste – and there are characteristics such as structure, texture and density that give a particular food and wine combination its 'mouthfeel'. But some combinations are definitely to be avoided. A highly refined and discreet wine for instance is wasted on a strong-tasting dish. Likewise, a fluid wine will seem thin in the company of a tightly textured, fleshy cut of meat. You can expect a few surprises along the way too. You will find in your search for the perfect match that certain dishes simply do not go with a very elegant wine; that the subtlest wines are often at their best with plain-cooked foods such as grilled meats. A wine that struck you as slightly unbalanced when you tasted it on its own might improve in the company of a certain dish. Some wines indeed are just not built for conventional tasting. Good examples are the Jura Vins Jaunes that can seem pungently aromatic on their own, but taste quite different with a piece of Comté cheese. What you notice then are subtle floral notes, aromas of walnuts, almonds and honey and a rich, complex texture.

Achieving a harmonious match does of course depend on good quality ingredients in the first place. You then have to consider their compatibility in terms of aroma, flavour and texture. The aromas should collude and never collide with or overpower the palate. The flavours (acidity, bitterness, sweetness, etc) should be complementary but never too much so. A sweet wine for instance should never be served with a sweet dessert. Likewise, a rather lively wine will tend to seem a bit dull alongside a lemony dish. The textures (fondant, tight, firm or fluid) must also be mutually compatible. A solid, four-square wine for example needs smooth, creamy sauces to balance its tannins.

Here again, we have a choice of possibilities. One is to look for a match based on a fusion of qualities, bringing together a wine and food with the same, mutually enhancing aromas. A Sauternes and an exotic fruit zabaglione, for example. Here you have a wine and food so intimately matched that they seem to merge in the mouth – it is almost impossible to distinguish one from the other. Alternatively, you can go for a marriage of opposites, relying on complementary qualities to emphasize the distinctions between them. Think of an old Pomerol with its notes of the forest floor and humus. Suppose you planned to serve it at a summer picnic – a challenging but not necessarily inappropriate choice, providing you get the food right. In such a case, you might look for a dish that rouses the palate, playing on a theme of fresh fruit sauce or dried tomatoes. But whatever you decide, do not lose sight of your goal, which is to obtain a matching blend of aroma and texture that creates a strong impact at the table and does in the event give real pleasure.

The questions that remain concern the order of serving, with a harmonious succession of dishes from the starter to the dessert. Whether you stick to the same wine throughout the meal or go for a series of ideal food and wine 'matches', remember once again that it is the overall impression that counts. No dish or wine should ever compare unfavourably with those that came before it. It used to be the rule that wines had to be served in order of age, starting with the youngest and finishing with the oldest, the best being kept for the cheese. In my experience however, and contrary to received opinion, cheese rarely brings out the best in wine – especially not an old red wine. Young, quite lively wines are in practice a better choice because their aromas are more of a match for the often somewhat robust aromas of cheese.

A few simple guidelines might be useful at this stage. When serving wines with a meal, you should start with the lightest (usually the youngest) and finish with the strongest (usually the oldest), except in the case of cheese (see above). As for the age-old question of whether to serve a white or a red wine, that's mostly a matter of common sense. Simply match the colour of the wine to the colour of the food and you are unlikely to go wrong. Your safest bet is to stick to white wines for white meat, poultry or fish (in a terrine, for instance) and red wines for darker meats and dark-fleshed poultry (such as guinea fowl or duck). Tuna, red mullet and other red-fleshed fish are equally good with red wine. This may not always be the most harmonious match but it does at least avoid the worst mistakes.

If you are serving only a single wine, there are many ways you can make it seem different as the meal progresses. Start by selecting your main dish – fish or meat in most cases – and pick a wine to match. Now decide on a starter that will bring out the qualities in the wine and last of all select your cheeses, avoiding any aromas that clash. You can also take advantage of the progressive changes in wine temperature and airing. Setting aside any preconceived ideas about wine and food combinations, imagine planning a meal entirely around a white wine. You would serve it chilled as an aperitif and with your starter. You would then allow it to warm in the glass for a while, so it had time to flesh out before the main dish. At the close of the meal, there would be no reason to change to a red wine for the cheese. Your white wine will by then be nicely aired and just the right temperature – proving a better match for a good selection of goat's cheeses than a red wine ever could.

If this all seems a bit complex, take a look at the following chapters. What you will find there are a wide variety of suggestions, each one highlighting a near-enough ideal food and wine match. For ease of use, the dishes are given in the order of serving, from starter to dessert. In each case, I have tried to show what

it is about a particular combination that makes it ideal. I have also given you options for substituting one wine for another, or one dish for another (should you prefer to stay with the same wine throughout the meal). I tell you how old the wine should be, the proper serving temperature and whether or not to decant it in advance. At the back of the book, by popular request, you will find the names and addresses of selected suppliers, indexed by name of appellation area.

If you get lost, simply refer to one of the two cross-referenced indexes. The first lists not only the dishes but also most of the ingredients that are likely to raise questions in your mind. Say you want a wine (or wines) to go with a strong-tasting ingredient like peppers, or a dish that is heavily laced with garlic. Simply look for 'pepper' or 'garlic'. The second index lists the appellations and includes a selection of suitable dishes. So if you were wondering what to serve with that Châteauneuf-du-Pape that's been sitting in your cellar for the past ten years, simply look up the relevant entry. You should find at least one suggestion that will fit the bill. For more information to get your culinary juices flowing, see the recipes presented on pages 153-161. Here you will discover how to create each of the dishes in this book.

I hope that what you will find along the way will surprise and delight you and rouse your gourmet soul. Because whatever the dictates of custom and culture, taste is always a matter of personal preference. People with a distinct penchant for one type of cuisine will naturally look for a wine with complementary qualities. Alternatively, if like me you are a wine lover first and foremost, you will start with the wine and seek a dish that best brings out its qualities. But whatever your taste, it's pleasure that comes first and the pleasures of the table in particular: a partnership of tastes for you to share and discover.

The flavour scale
The taste of the wine is represented on each page (top left-hand corner) by a colour scale, with a cursor to indicate the level of taste. The paler the colour, the lighter, tender and less complex the wine, usually meaning it is for early drinking. The darker the colour, the more powerful and complex the wine and the more suitable it is for aging.

POUILLY-FUME
smoked fish platter

AOC
Pouilly-Fumé
REGION
Loire
WHITE WINE
AREA
1,000ha
CULTIVAR
Sauvignon

Tightly textured, strongly flavoured fish such as smoked salmon, halibut or herring have an intense bouquet with hints of wooded aromas that make them more than a match for most wines.

A plate of smoked fish is a treat for all the senses. Those thin, translucent slices greet the nose with pungent aromas of fish smoked over beech-wood or oak, as the palate meanwhile succumbs to the melt-in-the-mouth sensation of succulent flesh.

It is well known that people in Scandinavian countries like to drink chilled aquavit or sometimes vodka with their smoked fish. Not a bad idea, this marriage of such violently contrasting opposites. But my personal preference would be a white wine, not too round or too fat, to avoid any clash of texture that might spoil the overall effect. For me, the perfect choice with smoked fish would be a very dry white wine, with a predominantly mineral bouquet and plenty of crispness, served slightly chilled but not cold. A Sancerre would be good but even better would be one of its close neighbours, a Pouilly-Fumé. As a visitor to the vineyard 20 years ago, I discovered then that wine growers there like to drink their Pouilly with oysters, small pieces of andouille (a type of chitterling sausage) and – this was what immediately took my fancy – slices of lightly smoked Loire salmon. A Pouilly has a strongly mineral quality, marked by distinctive notes of flint from the terroir, and a lively, nervous, almost trenchant quality. At the same time, it displays all the exuberant fruit of the Sauvignon grape, with flaunting aromas of blackcurrant buds combined with tantalizing lemony notes.

For perfect balance, it's best to pick a fairly young wine because as it ages a Pouilly-Fumé does tend to lose some of its thirst-quenching appeal. It becomes tamer if you like – more complex aromatically, more full-bodied and generous – and better suited to a dish of pikeperch or pike quenelles, garnished with asparagus tips.

Other dishes to go with this wine
With a 1-4 year old wine:
Seafood salad (cockles and mussels)
Fish terrine with baby vegetables
Grilled lobster or spiny lobster drizzled
  with lemon-flavoured olive oil
With a 4-10 year old wine:
Asparagus (served cold)
Pikeperch or pike quenelles in a
  white sauce
Dry goat's cheese (Chavignol de Sancerre)

Other wines to go with this dish
Sancerre
Menetou-Salon
Riesling Sec de Moselle
New Zealand Sauvignon
Blanc de Blancs Champagne (fairly young)
Aquavit or Vodka

The sommelier's selection
Château de Tracy
Didier Dagueneau
Domaine Redde
Domaine des Berthiers Dagueneau
Maison Guy Saget

CASSIS BLANC

white fish terrine with aioli sauce

AOC
Cassis
REGION
Provence
WHITE WINE
**This AOC also
produces
5% reds and
25% rosés**
AREA
**123ha given to
whites (total
170ha)**
CULTIVARS
**Mainly:
Marsanne
Pascal
Also:
Ugni Blanc
Clairette
Doucillon**

The first, highly delicate task is to create a harmonious blend of all the different ingredients in the terrine. The next step is to pick a wine that will marry well with the firm texture of the Mediterranean fish, the sweet flavour of the baby vegetables and the unmistakable fragrance of a raw garlic sauce.

This terrine is made of layers of fish – bass, gilt-head bream, red sea bream – alternating with baby vegetables – carrots and leeks – cut in julienne strips and preferably cooked al dente so as to contrast with the fluid texture of the aioli sauce. With this particular dish, I recommend a mild-flavoured, rather liquid sauce, with the lightest suggestion of raw garlic so as to avoid dulling the palate. The terrine itself calls for a fairly young wine, one creamy enough to offset the firmness of the fish pieces but mineral enough to overcome the persistence of the garlic. Serve it well chilled (around 9°C/48.2°F) to highlight the sweetness of the baby vegetables. Given the style of dish, I would choose a white wine from Cassis every time.

I love the white wines of Cassis, partly because I am a native of Provence myself, and partly because these wines have a unique personality that deserves to be better known. They owe their character to an ideally exposed vineyard overlooking the famous calanques of Cassis (rocky creeks), and a naturally cool microclimate found only on this stretch of the coast near Marseilles. It saddens me that these wines are mainly reserved for the bouillabaisses and bourrides (traditional fish soup with aioli) that are served on the waterfront. The first time I ever tasted a Cassis white wine with a white fish terrine and aioli was in fact in a Cassis restaurant – where I had originally intended to order a bouillabaisse! The blend of local products worked beautifully. A Cassis white wine has mineral notes of limestone and an immediate garrigue-like fruitiness that invite a variety of combinations. It is best drunk young (aged 2-3 years) as an aperitif or with the starter. In summer it makes a delicious accompaniment to grilled fish, while in winter I love it with shellfish such as mussels with garlic and parsley au gratin.

Other dishes to go with this wine
Fresh goat's cheese terrine, baby leeks
   and sun-dried tomatoes in olive oil
Seafood soufflé
Snails (cagoles) Provençale
Bouillabaisse and bourride
Grilled bass with fennel stems
   (but no Pastis!)
Cod parcels
Breaded whiting with lemon parsley butter
Courgettes au gratin, served hot or cold
Cassis free-range goat's cheese drizzled
   with olive oil

Other wines to go with this dish
Ajaccio Blanc
Savennières
Nuragus di Cagliari (Italy)
Grüner Veltliner Wachau (Austria)

The sommelier's selection
Château de Fontcreuse
Clos Sainte-Magdeleine
Clos Val Bruyère
Domaine du Bagnol
Domaine Saint-Louis

BOURGUEIL ROUGE
charcuterie platter

AOC
Bourgueil
REGION
Loire
RED WINE
**This AOC also
produces
3% rosés**
AREA
**1,250ha given
to reds (total
1,285ha)**
CULTIVARS
**Mainly:
Cabernet Franc
(known locally
as Breton)
Also:
Cabernet
Sauvignon**

Delicious though it is, charcuterie such as rillettes (potted mince), saucisson (dry sausage), andouille (a type of chitterling sausage) or cured ham can be a bit too rich and peppery – quite a challenge for most wines.

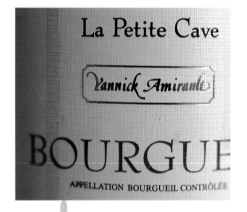

Finding a wine that goes well with charcuterie isn't as easy as you might think. First of all, you have to get the ambience right. Serving an overly complex wine with such basic peasant fare would be sheer bad taste. What you need instead is a fruity, thirst-quenching, easily quaffable character with a distinctly French feel. The only wine with the panache to carry it off is, to my mind, a Bourgueil.

The charcuterie/Bourgueil combination has become somewhat of an obsession with me. I associate it with happy times spent in the company of the actor Jean Carmet who did so love a glass of Bourgueil with his saucisson. It would be wrong to think of a Bourgueil as a 'minor' wine. It is a magnificent, simple but thoroughbred wine that comes at an affordable price and combines with an infinite variety of dishes. What's more, it has those thirst-quenching qualities that you need when serving andouille de Guéméné or rillettes. The rich texture of the charcuterie is complemented by the fruity, rounded wine with its aromas of blackcurrants and raspberries. At the same time, the smoky, spicy notes in the wine create an impression of great finesse, conjuring up warm images of gatherings round an open fire. A Bourgueil needs no decanting and is ready for drinking within 2-3 years. Served fairly cold (16°C/60.0°F) it has the stamina to hold centre stage throughout a meal but, being only moderate fleshy, will never overpower the flavours of fish or cheese, which it complements beautifully. Thanks to its personality and somewhat vegetal tannins, it also has the capacity to age well. In which case, I like to serve it at around 18°C (64.4°F) with pheasant or partridge barded with bacon en cocotte.

Other dishes to go with this wine
With a 2-3 year old wine:
Freshwater fish: pikeperch, pike or
conger eel in red wine sauce
Matelote (eel stewed in wine with onion
and herbs)
Free-range Loire chicken, garnished
with potatoes, onions and lardons
Quasi (rump of veal with peas
and lardons)
Cheese dishes:
Tartiflette au Reblochon (baked potatoes,
onions, bacon and Reblochon cheese)
Brie
Loire goat's cheese: Sainte-Maure,
Pyramide de Valençay
With a 5-8 year old wine:
Partridge or pheasant in cocotte

Other wines to go with this dish
Red wines:
Beaujolais
Côtes du Rhône-Villages
Vin de Corse – Calvi
White wines:
Chignin Bergeron and other Savoie whites
Beaujolais Blanc
Vouvray Sec

The sommelier's selection
Domaine Yannick Amirault
Domaine Druet
Domaine Gambier
Maison Lame Delille Bouchard

BEAUJOLAIS ROUGE
chicken liver terrine

AOC
Beaujolais
REGION
Burgundy
RED WINE
**This AOC also
produces
1% rosés and 1%
whites**
AREA
**22,500ha given to
reds (total
23,000ha)**
CULTIVAR
Gamay

The fresh, thirst-quenching character of Beaujolais Nouveau makes for an easy match here, the wine's fluidity complementing the mousse-like texture of the chicken liver terrine.

For me, there is something rustic and entirely unpretentious about the harmony of a Beaujolais Nouveau with a chicken liver terrine. On the one hand, you have a dish that everybody knows, with its hint of bitterness, a light, almost frothy texture and sweetly spicy notes. On the other hand, you have a wine that almost everybody knows, with its nose of boiled sweets and redcurrants and a palate recalling the lushness of strawberries and raspberries.

Every year in late November, you can expect to find a bottle of Beaujolais Nouveau on practically every table in France. People mainly drink it with charcuterie but I think it shows best with a melt-in-the-mouth terrine and a hunk of crusty farmhouse loaf. Serve the wine chilled but not cold (around 12-13°C/53.6-55.4°F) and make sure the terrine isn't too peppery since this match depends on mild flavours. Otherwise, this combination works a treat.

Fashionable trends aside, Beaujolais wines deserve far greater recognition than their somewhat simplistic label suggests. There are in fact 10 Beaujolais crus, all of them yielding extremely elegant wines that represent the finest expression of the Gamay grape. Having often had the pleasure of tasting a 10 year old Morgon or Saint-Amour, I can tell you that there is nothing in the least bit 'simplistic' about them. Served at around 16°C (60.8°F), they are perfectly delicious with more ambitious fare: feathered game for instance, such as pheasant or partridge roasted in its own juices.

Other dishes to go with this wine
Charcuterie: pâtés, rillettes, saucisson
Grilled andouillette
Roast guinea fowl or chicken, with a fresh
  vegetable ratatouille
Goat's cheese: Boutons de culotte from
  the Mâconnais and Beaujolais areas
Red berry desserts: red fruit soup
  (strawberries, cherries, raspberries)
  garnished with strawberry sorbet

Other wines to go with this dish
Côtes du Forez
Côte Roannaise
Saint-Pourçain
Vin de Savoie (Gamay)
Bugey (Gamay)
Grignolino del Piemonte (Italy)

The sommelier's selection
Domaine des Terres Dorées
Domaine Pivot Jean-Charles
Domaine Croix Charnay
Domaine Piron
Maison Dubœuf

SAVIGNY-LES-BEAUNE ROUGE
parsley ham

AOC
Savigny-Lès-
Beaune
REGION
Burgundy
RED WINE
This AOC also
produces
10% whites
AREA
315ha given to
reds (total 350ha)
CULTIVAR
Pinot Noir

Finding a wine to go with this typically Burgundian dish is not as easy as you might think, due to the uneven mixture of ingredients in the parsley ham: whole pieces of meat, plus pungently vegetal herbs and a semi-solid, semi-liquid aspic.

Not an easy match to pull off, this one. The vegetal flavours of the dish would normally call for a wine with freshness and crispness, but one that isn't so dense as to stifle the texture of the meat or the 'slipperiness' of the aspic. What you need then is a wine that isn't overly heavy. Likewise, the ham should go easy on the garlic and pepper so as to maintain an overall sense of harmony. The delicacy of the dense, succulent meat should go unnoticed at the outset, concealed by the flavours of the parsley and herbs that are steeped in the aspic. A tannic or overly powerful red is plainly out of the question – which is why they traditionally serve parsley ham in Burgundy with a … white wine.

How surprising then that it was in Savigny itself that I first came across the more unorthodox red wine combination. This was back in 1980, when I had gone to Savigny to taste the wines made by the late Simon Bize, an exceptional wine grower who also loved to cook. It was Simon who introduced me to the taste of parsley ham combined with his own Savigny-Lès-Beaune – a perfectly harmonious match if ever there was one. I love the unique style of the Savigny. This is an honest, light, supple and elegant wine, born of a mildly volcanic terroir, that combines fresh raspberry notes with just enough tannins and fluidity to avoid dilution. Thanks to these original qualities, it can adapt to a wide variety of dishes, whether eggs en meurette (poached in red wine sauce) or roast meat. For parsley ham, I would choose a young wine (around five years old) served at 17°C (62.6°F). With older vintages, I would prefer a pork fillet mignon with carrots and perhaps a spicy touch of cumin to highlight the spiciness in the wine.

Other dishes to go with this wine
With a 3-5 year old wine:
Mushroom and herb raviolis in
 winegrower sauce
Eggs en meurette (red wine sauce with
 bacon, onions and mushrooms)
Pikeperch in red butter sauce, fresh tagliatelle
 and mushrooms with garlic and parsley
Grilled tuna steak with herbs
Spit-roasted leg of lamb
Spit-roasted ham sauce vigneronne
Cheeses: Tomme du Morvan,
 Soumaintrain Frais, Chaource.
 With a 10 year old wine:
Pork fillet mignon with carrots and cumin

Other wines to go with this dish
Chablis Premier Cru
Pouilly-Fuissé
Pernand-Vergelesses Blanc

The sommelier's selection
Daniel Largeot
Domaine Chandon de Brialles
Domaine Rapet
Domaine Simon Bize et Fils

PACHERENC DU VIC-BILH MOELLEUX
duck foie gras cooked in a terrine

AOC
Pacherenc du Vic-Bilh
REGION
South West France
WHITE
MOELLEUX WINE
This AOC also produces 40% dry whites
AREA
220ha
CULTIVARS
Mainly (local cultivars): Arrufiac Petit and Gros Manseng Courbu Also (Bordeaux cultivars): Sauvignon Sémillon

I like to serve whole foie gras sprinkled with sea salt and lightly garnished with fruit such as prune chutney, thinly sliced dried apples or quince jelly. The wine to go with it must supply a combination of sweetness and freshness.

There are so many sorts of duck foie gras that it's impossible to generalize. But one thing is certain: the sweet wines traditionally drunk with foie gras in South West France are now just as customary elsewhere. It would be hard to think of a better match. A succulent duck foie gras, with its game-like taste and hint of bitterness and spice, seems just made for a wine that is smooth but not oversweet – one that combines a certain youthful freshness with more mature notes of candied fruits.

My first-ever visit to the Madiran region was back in 1984 when I went there to taste red wines before stopping over in a farmhouse inn. As I sat down to dinner, the landlady placed a whole terrine on my table and my first thought was to order a Sauternes. This drew a sharp protest from my host who suggested I try instead a local wine, the Pacherenc du Vic-Bilh. It proved a revelation. Pacherenc du Vic-Bilh, from the Ardour valley, is a sweet but never cloying wine made from cultivars specific to the region. Despite its remarkable smoothness, the wine retains a surprising freshness with distinctive notes of orchard fruits (apples, pears, plums, etc). Quite like a Jurançon, not as enchanting as a Sauternes, but with quite as much refinement as the great sweet wines. This is a wine off the beaten track and as such it makes for an ideal if somewhat unorthodox match with a duck foie gras. Choose a wine around five years old, served at 10°C (50.4°F) so as to bring out its freshness. A young Pacherenc du Vic-Bilh is best with fresh fruit, while a more mature wine goes magnificently with some desserts, especially nutty ones. Note that chocolate or red berries are best avoided.

Other wines to go with this dish
Jurançon Moelleux
Sauternes
Barsac
Cérons
Alsace Tokay-Pinot Gris
   Sélection de Grains Nobles
Vin de Constance (South Africa)

Other dishes to go with this wine
Blue cheese made from sheep's milk
Sorbets: mango, pineapple, apple, pear,
   banana, litchi
Frozen nougat
Nutty patisseries (pistachios, almonds,
   hazelnuts)
Four-fruit dessert based on citrus fruit

The sommelier's selection
Château Bouscassé
Château d'Aydie
Château Laffitte-Teston
Producteurs de Plaimont

CONDRIEU

warm asparagus in gribiche sauce

AOC
Condrieu
REGION
Rhône Valley
DRY WHITE WINE
**This AOC also
produces
moelleux wines**
AREA
100ha
CULTIVAR
Viognier

This unusual dish is a bit of a challenge due to the contrast of textures and flavours. The stringiness of the asparagus, together with its vegetal taste and watery consistency, rule out any strongly flavoured sauce – which is why asparagus is generally served au naturel. It is best combined with a rounded, supple wine.

For a wine lover like me, finding a good match for asparagus is always a challenge. To start with, you need to know how the asparagus is to be served, whether on its own or as a garnish, cold or hot, with vinaigrette, a mayonnaise or with a sauce. Try as I might, I have rarely encountered a wine that didn't take on an unpleasantly metallic taste when drunk with asparagus. Then I discovered this unlikely combination of warm asparagus in gribiche sauce with Condrieu wine.

Condrieu, made from Viognier grapes, is a rare gem of a wine from the Rhône Valley. In its dry white incarnation, it is usually served with the starter and, as any gourmet will tell you, it has a particular affinity for asparagus. The vegetal tendencies of the asparagus are nicely tempered by the explosively fruity (fresh grapes, apricots) and floral (violets) aromas, in a wine that combines a velvety touch with good bite. The first time I ever tasted this combination, the gribiche sauce had actually been destined for another dish. I was already fond of Condrieu and asparagus with vinaigrette, or with a delicately flavoured citrus mousse sauce, but this was something else altogether. Daring too, given the striking mixture of ingredients in the sauce (hard-boiled egg yokes, mustard, vinegar, capers, gherkins) and its peculiarly smooth/granular/crunchy consistency. Smooth because it is an emulsion, granular because it contains chopped hard-boiled egg white, and crunchy by virtue of the coarse-ground condiments. However complex it may sound, the combination works beautifully with a supple, nicely rounded Condrieu that will retain all of its freshness after 2-3 years' aging. For an original touch, you can also serve Condrieu with warm asparagus in the classic style.

Other wines to go with this dish
Chablis Premier Cru
Pessac-Léognan Blanc Sec
Alsace Muscat Sec
Savennières
Wines to go with cold asparagus
Alsace Riesling
Pouilly-Fumé
Hawke's Bay Sauvignon (New Zealand)
Wachau Riesling (Austria)

Other dishes to go with this wine
　With a 2-3 year old wine:
Potted shrimps on toast, as an aperitif
Eggs mimosa
Pan-sautéed back of pikeperch with
　risotto and asparagus tips
Pike quenelles with Nantua sauce and
　white rice
　With a 5-7 year old wine:
Chicken with crayfish

The sommelier's selection
Domaine Cuilleron
Domaine Vernay
Domaine Gaillard
Domaine Perret
Domaine Villard

ARBOIS ROUGE
poached eggs en meurette

AOC
Arbois
REGION
The Jura
RED WINE
This AOC also produces rosé and white wines, Vins de Paille and Vins Jaunes
AREA
450ha given to reds (total 920ha)
CULTIVARS
Mainly (local cultivars): Trousseau Poulsard Also: Pinot Noir

Versatile they may be, but eggs tend to bring out a metallic, even bitter taste in wine. Cooking them in a wine sauce (en meurette) gets round the problem, using the sauce to create an impression of harmony.

Making this dish successfully does require a certain amount of skill. The egg must be perfectly cooked so as to bring out the contrast between the creaminess of the yoke and the firmness of the white, poached in water. The butter-wine sauce meanwhile adds an extra velvetiness.

It's when it comes to choosing the wine that things start to get difficult. Or to be more precise, the problem is the egg and the answer is the wine. In Burgundy where eggs en meurette are a traditional favourite, they usually pick a rounded red that is neither overly alcoholic nor too delicate. An Arbois Rouge may not be so classical but to my mind it does just as well. It was the restaurateur Jean-Paul Jeunet who first introduced me to the idea of Arbois wine with eggs en meurette. I was in the Jura on business at the time (presiding over the annual Percée du Vin Jaune wine-opening celebrations). Moments after the first taste, I could see that this was a winning combination of simplicity and refinement. With its notes of red fruits and spices and just a touch of leather, the Jura wine has a personality strong enough to match the egg, while the palate adds a very welcome freshness. With this dish, serve the wine on the cold side (around 16°C/60.8°F) so as to bring out its typically Jura mineral character. When making the meurette sauce with Arbois wine, bear in mind that for a seamless blend of flavours, the consistency of the sauce must pick up on the game-like, kirsch-like aromas in the wine.

Other dishes to go with this wine
Poultry or game terrine
Dried meat such as viande des Grisons
Mixed salad leaves with smoked duck
    breast fillet and garlic croutons
Guinea fowl with cabbage
Pot-au-feu
Lapin chasseur with champignons de Paris
Cheese: Morbier du Jura
Spice crème brûlée (vanilla, cinnamon,
    allspice)

Other wines to go with this dish
Côtes du Jura Rouge
Savigny-Lès-Beaune Rouge
Monthélie Rouge
Auxey-Duresses Rouge
Bourgogne-Hautes-Côtes de Nuits Rouge
Irancy

The sommelier's selection
Domaine de la Pinte
Domaine Overnoy
Domaine Rolet Père et Fils
Domaine André et Mireille Tissot

VIN DE SAVOIE CHIGNIN BERGERON
snails with garlic and herbs

AOC
Vin de Savoie Chignin Bergeron
REGION
Savoie
WHITE WINE
AREA
Total 1,725ha for the Vin de Savoie AOC
CULTIVAR
Roussanne, known locally as Bergeron

It is often said that the snail is just a vehicle for garlic and herbs, and has little or no taste of its own. Truth is, it has a delicate taste that too much garlic will smother. A mineral-tasting wine will bring out all of its hidden potential.

Snails are much sought after - by some, but by no means all – for their very particular, not to say chewy, consistency. They are prepared in various ways, whether in puff pastry with a herby sauce or – and this is the most usual way – in their shells, with garlic and parsley butter. Another method is to mince the parsley with a pinch of sorrel before combining the butter and garlic. It is important not to over-do the garlic: there should be just enough to liven the taste buds but not so much as to stun the palate. Getting the garlic right is the key to unlocking the bouquet of flavours created by the snails, the herbs and … the wine.

With snails, avoid anything too overblown or overly alcoholic. What you want is a fairly lively, youngish wine, served slightly chilled and still retaining good fruit character. It was when I was a student at the Ecole Hôtelière de Grenoble that I first worked on Savoie wines, and I remember what a problem we had with the white Chignin Bergeron. For all its qualities – excellent reputation, tangible texture, lovely length, respectable density – it hardly seemed to go with anything. It was only when we tried it with snails that we really got a sense of harmony. The wine was still young, with notes of orchard fruits (pears and apricots) and a slightly acidulous, pulpy, mineral quality. I've remained faithful to this combination ever since. If you choose an unwooded wine and serve it lightly chilled (8-9°C/46-48°F), you have a perfect match: a fruity taste to make the garlic barely noticeable and the mineral qualities to bring out the delicate flavours in the snail. Each mouthful leaves your mouth deliciously refreshed.

Other wines to go with this dish
White wines:
Mâcon-Villages
Red wines:
Alsace Pinot Noir
Menetou-Salon
Irancy
Bourgogne Epineuil
Fiefs Vendéens

Other dishes to go with this wine
Ham, mountain saucisson and other
   Savoie charcuterie
Cheese fondue and tartiflette Savoy-style
Cheeses: Tomme de Savoie, Reblochon

The sommelier's selection
Domaine André et Michel Quénard
Domaine Raymond Quénard
Domaine Louis Magnin

CHATEAU-CHALON
comté cheese and walnut pie

AOC
Château Chalon
REGION
Jura
WHITE WINE
(Vin Jaune)
AREA
45ha
CULTIVAR
Savagnin

All the art of this dish lies in striking the right balance of flavours, between the pungently aromatic hot cheese, the slightly bitter walnuts and the richly buttery puff pastry. This apparently simple dish has a boldness of flavour that is more than a match for most wines.

Long before it reaches the table, this cheese pie fills the air with its warm aromas, of melted Comté wrapped in buttery flaky pastry. But having announced its arrival, the mysterious pie is in no hurry to reveal its contents. What lies inside will remain a secret until you bite into that crispy layer of pastry - and discover a filling with the consistency of a cheese-laden Béchamel sauce dotted with fragments of walnut.

The variety of sensations aroused by this tantalizing dish reaches new heights with the arrival of the wine. Marshalling all of these different elements is as much a question of pitch as flavour. With such a mouth-filling first taste, it takes a full-bodied wine of exceptional persistence to slip harmoniously into what little space remains.

To my mind, the only wines capable of rising to this challenge are the Jura Vins Jaunes, and the Château-Chalon in particular. I first discovered Vins Jaunes when I was just starting out as a sommelier and I remember how disconcerting they seemed. They are made from

the Savagnin grape and cask-aged for six years and three months without ullage (no topping-up to replace evaporation). In the course of this time, the wine develops a film of yeasts that limits oxidation and gives it a very particular flavour. Everything about the Vins Jaunes takes time, from the 10 years or so required to make them to the time it takes for you to get to know them. You can spend an entire evening just savouring their bouquet, then tasting them sip by sip, saving those last few drops for the after-dinner conversation.

A Château-Chalon is a prince among Vins Jaunes: dense, delicate and powerful, with fragrant aromas of walnuts – that go well with the pie – curry, citrus, honey and dried rose petals. Despite its age, it retains a very honest, incisive, almost austere side. This is a complex, full-bodied wine with good presence. It also has a slightly heady quality that strikes a near-perfect balance with the hot Comté. To make a main dish of this entrée, simply add some diced smoked ham to the filling – its aromas will serve as an elegant reminder of the spicy smokiness acquired by the wine in the course of its long aging.

Other dishes go with this wine
Andalusian Gazpacho
Curried, roasted Dublin Bay prawns, on a
    bed of spinach with sesame lace biscuits
Bresse hen in Vin Jaune
Curried sauté of veal
Meat and fruit curry (sliced almonds,
    pineapple) with rice

Other wines to go with this dish
Arbois Vin Jaune
L'Etoile (Jaune)
Côtes du Jura (Jaune)
Gaillac Vin de Voile
Fino Sherry (Spain)

The sommelier's selection
Domaine Jean-Marie Courbet
Domaine Jean Macle
Domaine Jacques et Barbara Durand-Perron

L'ETOILE BLANC
beaufort soufflé

AOC
L'Etoile
REGION
Jura
WHITE WINE
This AOC also
produces
Vins Jaunes
AREA
79ha
CULTIVARS
Savagnin
Chardonnay

This pungently aromatic soufflé must be served piping hot, with a wine that is not so cold as to create a sharp contrast in temperature.

Your guests sit patiently waiting for the soufflé to be perfectly cooked. To make their wait more endurable, you serve the wine and leave it to warm in the glasses. At last, the soufflé makes its entrance, wafting into the room on a wave of succulent aromas, with burnished, nut-brown tones to delight the eye and a taste so intense it is worth burning your tongue for. Last but by no means least in this ode to indulgence comes the sensual, mousse-like texture, radiating with palate-coating flavour. A soufflé is a feast for all the senses.

Such an explosion of sensations calls for a wine with a powerful character. Red wines, with one or two exceptions, should be avoided here since the eggs and milk in the soufflé might make them seem slightly bitter. As to white wines, there is one in particular from the Jura region that makes an ideal match: L'Etoile, a wine from a little-known appellation that owes its name (and mineral qualities) to the deposits of star-shaped fossils found throughout the vineyard. L'Etoile is made from the Savagnin grape (also used to make the Vins Jaunes) and is characteristic of its cultivar and terroir: golden yellow colour, aromas of green walnuts and almonds, curry or nutmeg on the nose, lots of good, fresh body. A 4-5 year old wine stands a particularly good chance with a soufflé. It has enough persistence to survive even the richest of flavours but all the freshness required to bring out the soufflé's airy, mousse-like texture. Served at around 14°C (57.2°F) it will retain all of its mineral edge, enhancing the intensity of the hot cheese flavours.

Other wines to go with this wine
Côtes du Jura
Arbois
Rully Blanc (5 years +)
Mercurey Blanc (5 years +)
Mâcon Blanc (5 years +)
Viré-Clessé (5 years +)
Hermitage Blanc (10 years +)

Other dishes to go with this wine
Mildly spicy shrimp zakouski, or cumin
   seed pastries (appetizers)
Mildly spicy seafood soufflé with saffron
   or curry
Saffron lobster
Bresse hen in a cream sauce with morel
   mushrooms and fresh pasta
Laguiole aligot (cheesy mashed potatoes)
Cheeses: Comté or Beaufort
Caramelised walnut tart

The sommelier's selection
Château de l'Étoile
Domaine Geneletti
Domaine de Montbourgeau

POMEROL
foie gras and truffle turnover

AOC
Pomerol
REGION
Bordeaux
RED WINE
AREA
800ha
CULTIVARS
Mainly:
Merlot
Cabernet
Sauvignon
Also:
Cabernet Franc
Malbec

An exceptional, delectable, aromatically gifted dish in which the aroma of truffles must dominate all other flavours.

Truffles, being as rare as they are eye-wateringly expensive, naturally deserve a wine that is the apotheosis of refinement. It was leading French chef Marc Meneau who first introduced me to this particular delicacy: a divinely flaky, impossibly light turnover tucked around a truffle with just enough foie gras to keep the whole thing moist. From the moment it reached the table, the air was filled with aromas of mushroom and that all-pervasive fragrance of foie gras – such a treat for the nose that indulging the taste buds is almost an irrelevance … As to the wine, Marc had no hesitation in picking a Bordeaux (even though his own establishment is near Vézelay, Burgundy). The choice was a nicely aged Pomerol with truffle aromas that went beautifully with those in the turnover.

Pomerol and truffles make an obvious – and usually successful – match. As it ages, a Pomerol acquires thoroughbred aromas that echo the intensely delicate fragrance of a truffle. Combining one with the other is as logical as it is symbolic, conjuring up images of celebration, elegance and subtlety. But the combination must also allow for the creaminess of the foie gras and the airy consistency of the puff pastry. Getting the balance just right is essential to avoid masking those aromas of humus, forest-floor and tobacco that you find in a great Pomerol. You are best off with a fairly mature Pomerol (10-15 years old), decanted beforehand and served at a temperature of 17-18°C (62.6-64.4°F). Decanting also gives you a chance to admire the wine's lovely, nearly brown garnet tones, that recall the golden shades of the puff pastry.

Other wines to go with this dish
Red wine:
Fairly mature, Châteauneuf-du-Pape
(10 years old)
Slightly moelleux white wines:
Jurançon Vendanges Tardives
Petite Arvine (Valois, Switzerland)

Other dishes to go with this wine
Warm, pan-sautéed foie gras
Truffles cooked in hot embers
Pigeon pie (pastilla)
Feathered game - pheasant, dove,
woodcock – in its juice or in a pie
Tournedos Rossini with ceps
Cantal Entre-Deux cheese
Milk chocolate tart with chestnut ice cream

The sommelier's selection
Clos du Clocher
Château Croix de Gay
Château La Conseillante
Château L'Église-Clinet
Château Lafleur
Château Le Bon Pasteur
Château Mazeyres
Château Petit-Village
Château Trotanoy
Vieux Château Certan

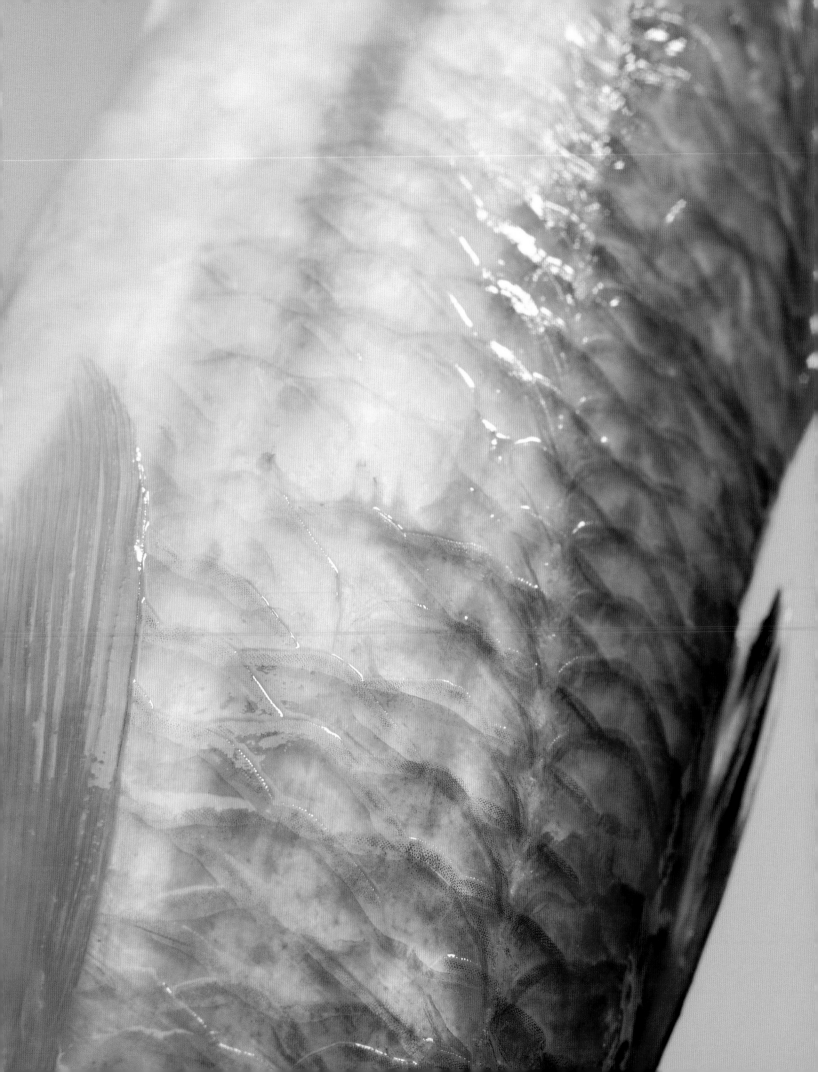

ALSACE RIESLING
seafood platter

AOC
Alsace Riesling
REGION
Alsace
DRY WHITE WINE
**This AOC also
produces
moelleux wines**
AREA
3,350ha
CULTIVAR
Riesling

The appeal of this dish lies in the variety of taste and tactile sensations aroused by so many different sorts of seafood. Such distinguished company calls for a wine that will harmonize with the variety in the dish.

Choice is the essence of a gorgeous seafood platter. There are oysters of every description: fattened and non-fattened, flat or creuse, fine de claire or belon. Then there are the other molluscs (raw mussels, for instance), other forms of shellfish (periwinkles, whelks, round clams, cockles …) and the small crustaceans (shrimps and Dublin Bay prawns). Such a multitude of tastes and textures is a treat for the seafood lover, but it does call for a discerning choice of wine. This dish would normally require an honest fruity, white wine, preferably dry and with good mineral edge – so nothing too rounded, wooded or over-aged. There are a number of possibilities, but most go better with one ingredient than with the others.

Personally, I think an Alsace Riesling is invariably the best choice with this dish. As a young sommelier, I once worked in a restaurant in Paris (the Brasserie Lorraine) where we used to serve seafood platter every day. I had plenty of opportunity to try it with different wines, but only the Riesling had what I was looking for: noble origins, elegance, breeding and undeniable personality. It is also unusually cooperative with this particular dish. A youngish Riesling, served chilled (7-8°C/44.6-46.4°F), has as much affinity for an acid, moistly fresh fattened oyster as for a briny tasting fine de claire, a firm, plump whelk or a delicate, somewhat flaccid raw mussel. An Alsace Riesling, I would say, is the only wine that chimes to perfection with the variety of flavours in a seafood platter.

Other wines to go with this dish
    White wines:
Chablis
Muscadet
Sancerre
Entre-Deux-Mers
Côteaux du Languedoc
Picpoul-de-Pinet
Paarl Chenin Blanc (South Africa)
    Red wines:
Saint-Nicolas-de-Bourgueil
Alsace Pinot Noir (young)

Other dishes to go with this wine
Raw oysters
White sausage with apple
Alsace charcuterie, warm saucisson
Alsace sauerkraut
Dishes to go with an Alsace Grand Cru Riesling
Lobster in cream sauce
Fish (bass, turbot, John Dory) with
   lemon butter

The sommelier's selection
Domaine Ostertag
Domaine Schueller
Maison Léon Beyer

MUSCADET DE SEVRE-ET-MAINE
mouclade (mussels in a cream sauce)

AOC
Muscadet
REGION
Loire
WHITE WINE
AREA
**13,000ha for the
AOC overall
(Sèvre et Maine,
Côteaux de la
Loire, Côtes
de Grand-Lieu)**
CULTIVAR
**Melon Blanc
(known locally as
Muscadet)**

This recipe from Nantes is a variation on the mussels theme so popular throughout Western France. It includes a large number of ingredients that must remain discreet so as not to deaden the powerfully iodized flavour of the mussels. The wine must achieve the same objective.

Of all the thousand different ways to prepare mussels, a mouclade in particular is a real feast for the eyes: a glorious extravaganza of colour with the yellowish orange of the mussel flesh making a striking contrast to the iridescent black of the shell and the pale tones of the cream sauce, with its smattering of chopped parsley. Note however that the mussels should never be drowned in sauce. The sauce – made with garlic, parsley, butter, celery salt, curry, fresh cream and white wine – should be thick enough to coat the mussels but not so thick as to dampen their briny flavour. That taste of the sea likewise determines the choice of wine: white, very dry and not too lively. A Muscadet, usually drunk young and well chilled, is one that fits the bill perfectly. It makes a logical combination with the mouclade since both are from the same terroir. What's more, being no stranger to the sea itself, a Muscadet highlights the iodised flavours of the dish. It too has that hint of the sea born of vines kissed by Atlantic spume and spray.

The Muscadet AOC is too big to claim excellence in all that it produces. But thanks to the efforts of certain winegrowers, some of its wines are better than their reputation suggests. I also know from experience that there are some excellent Muscadet vintage wines. Back in 1983 when I was doing my military service in the region, my father came to see me and took me to lunch at the Villa Mon Rêve in Nantes. The owner was the proud proprietor of a handsome collection of vintage wines, and to this day I am filled with emotion when I recall the Muscadet 1961 that he served us that day with a Brittany lobster in aromatic broth.

Other wines to go with this dish
Pouilly-sur-Loire
Vin de Savoie Ripaille
Bordeaux Sec
Fiefs Vendéens Blanc

Other dishes to go with this wine
With a 2-3 year old wine:
Serve as an aperitif
Peeled shrimp
Raw oysters
With a 5-6 year old wine (or more for great vintages):
Pikeperch or pike with white butter sauce

The sommelier's selection
Château de la Preuille
Château La Ragotière
Domaine de l'Écu
Domaine de la Louveterie
Domaine Luneau Papin

COTES DE PROVENCE ROSE
oursinade (sea urchins)

AOC
Côtes de
Provence
REGION
Provence
ROSE WINE
This AOC also
produces
15% reds and
5% whites
AREA
15,350ha given to
rosés (total
19,200ha)
CULTIVARS
Mainly:
Grenache
Cinsault
Syrah
Mourvèdre
Also:
Tibouren
Carignan
Cabernet-
Sauvignon

An oursinade is a part of the Provencal way of life – spending the day sailing down the rocky creeks or calanques off the coast of Marseilles, Cassis or Carry, eating sea urchins freshly plucked from the rocks.

A sea urchin is a rare delicacy. Few people today have the opportunity to go urchin fishing themselves and, because sea urchins travel badly, you hardly ever find them in France outside local markets. But what a treat they are for anyone lucky enough to eat them! Sea urchin roe, for a native of Provence like me, is a feast for all the senses. I love its bright, more or less orangey tones. I love the texture of those tiny grains of roe and their exquisitely iodised flavour.

But I don't like white wines with sea urchins. They seem to break up those little grains, not bind them together – something a more generous rosé does so well. And where better than Provence, the land of the rosé, to find the wine we want? There is a different style of rosé there for every appellation (Bandol, Palette, Côteaux Varois, Côtes de Provence and many others). What they all have in common is a taste of the summer and an affinity for Provençal cooking.

My favourite rosé with sea urchins is as always a youngish Côtes de Provence (mainly made from Cinsault and Syrah grapes). Whatever its warmth, this is a wine that never loses its light, fruity, acidulous qualities. Its mineral edge and notes of springtime flowers provide just the right foil for the briny-tasting sea urchin. Choose a young wine, served chilled, and take it along with you when you go fishing for the urchins. As you take the bottle from the cool box, you can feast your eyes on that tantalizingly cool vapour formed by the tiny droplets of moisture around the glass. Enjoy the lovely harmony of the prettily coloured wine and the warm, orangey roe. Sea urchins and Côtes de Provence wine are more than a good match – they are a way of life.

Other wines to go with this dish
Côteaux du Languedoc Rosé
Beaujolais Rosé
Marsannay Rosé
Sancerre and Loire rosés based
   on the Pinot grape
Penedes rosés (Spain)

Other dishes to go with this wine
Fish or poultry terrine
   with Provencal vegetables
Octopus salad with olive oil
   and balsamic vinegar
Seafood rice salad
Grilled pepper salad
Aubergine caviar
Grilled rock fish (red mullet,
   gilt-head bream)
Banon cheese with toast

The sommelier's selection
Château Barbeyrolles
Château des Garcinières
Château les Valentines
Château Sainte-Roseline
Domaine de Saint-Ser
Mas de Cadenet

PALETTE BLANC

roasted lobster with mild spices

AOC
Palette
REGION
Provence
WHITE WINE
This AOC also
produces
25% reds and
15% rosés
AREA
14ha given to
whites (total
36ha)
CULTIVARS
Mainly:
Clairette
Also:
Ugni Blanc
Grenache Blanc
Muscat Blanc
Terret-Bourret
Piquepoul
Aragnan
Pascal
Colembard

Other wines to go with this dish
White wines:
Châteauneuf-du-Pape
Hermitage
Rully
Puligny-Montrachet
Arbois
Pessac-Léognan
Alsace Tokay-Pinot Gris
Friuli Chardonnay (Italy)
Rueda (Spain)
Maule Valley Chardonnay (Chile)
Marlborough Chardonnay (New Zealand)
Red wines:
NB not recommended unless the dish has
    been deglazed with a Vin Doux Naturel
    (Banyuls or Maury)
Côtes du Roussillon
Côteaux du Languedoc

This dish is renowned for its delicacy but the recipe requires patience and skill. The lobster pieces in particular must be roasted to perfection so as to concentrate the juices in the sauce. Such fine cuisine deserves a thoroughbred wine.

Other dishes to go with this wine
Halibut or smoked trout salad
Bouillabaisse and bourride
Veal medallions in paprika cream
Chicken with garlic cloves

Lobster and Dublin Bay prawns are the most noble of all the crustaceans. They are mainly served as festive fare, preferably in the winter months when people have time for such difficult recipes. When preparing this dish, I recommend you slice the lobster tail (steeped but shell on) into medallions then sauté them in olive oil. The carcasses should be cooked separately beforehand then crushed in a frying pan, straining the juices and setting them aside for the sauce. Once the medallions are cooked, deglaze the pan with wine (preferably the Palette that you plan to serve at table), season the sauce with a pinch of paprika or allspice and thicken with a dollop of cream. A lobster prepared in this way will retain all of its qualities: firm flesh (without that flabby tendency sometimes seen in poached lobster) and authentic flavour, subtly highlighted by the sauce.

Such a refined dish deserves a great white wine. What first springs to mind is a Burgundy, which would of course do very well. But a Palette would be far more original. This unique wine is a particular favourite of mine, recalling many warm personal memories. Intensely Mediterranean and rigorously crafted, a Palette Blanc displays all the character of an exceptional terroir near Aix-en-Provence. The vines here are planted on north-facing slopes that give the Palette freshness. The Langesse limestone contributes fine mineral qualities while the Clairette grape adds unrivalled expression. A Palette Blanc is a rare wine due to the small size of its AOC. With lobster, it should be served at around 12°C (53.6°F) so as not to stun the wine's aromas by over-chilling. Its texture, strength, breeding and density, with jam-like notes from the time spent on wood, make it an ideal match for lobster meat in an intensely flavoured sauce.

The sommelier's selection
Château Crémade
Château Simone

CORTON-CHARLEMAGNE
crayfish in aromatic broth

AOC
Corton-Charlemagne
REGION
Burgundy
WHITE WINE
AREA
50ha
CULTIVAR
Chardonnay

There is nothing quite like the finesse of crayfish, a fast disappearing delicacy that should be cooked as simply as possible. It gives of its best with a great white wine.

Preparing the broth for the crayfish couldn't be easier. Simply dice the vegetables (carrots and onions) then combine with the mixed herbs (thyme, bay leaf, parsley), garlic clove and shallot, white wine, water and just enough zest of citrus (lemon and grapefruit) to add sharpness. Then leave the broth to reduce for a good 30 minutes before plunging in the crayfish. This is when it gets difficult because the meat has to be cooked just right so as to remain moist and succulent. But the crayfish must also stay intact. They definitely taste better that way even if it does mean using your fingers …

Which brings us to the wine and the problems of holding a glass with sauce-stained fingers. Essentially this is a question of doing things in the right order, starting with a sip of wine, followed by a few crayfish. Then pause for a while, only tasting the wine again as you are about to finish your plate. Eating with your fingers may seem a bit crude, but rest assured: crayfish in aromatic broth with a Corton-Charlemagne is the height of refinement. Crayfish deserves a great white wine and this particularly generous but not overly mellow wine is a perfect match. A Corton-Charlemagne is beyond question one of the princes of the Côte de Beaune wines. What I particularly love about this Burgundy cru is its uncompromising honesty and consistent balance over time. It is full-bodied, fresh and sharply mineral, but also austere, long and intensely aromatic. It does however take time to express itself and can seem a bit mean if tasted too young. With crayfish, you need a Corton-Charlemagne that has aged for at least five years. Providing you leave it to breathe in the decanter and serve it at the right temperature (around 11°C (51.8°F), its density, notes of exotic fruits and slightly nutty aromas will complement the flavours of the crayfish.

Other dishes to go with this wine
    With a 5-10 year old wine:
Cold or hot lobster or spiny lobster in
    aromatic broth
Oven-roast turbot or John Dory, with
    citrus sauce and white rice
Sole Meunière
    With a 10-15 year old wine:
Roast Bresse chicken with
    sautéed mushrooms
Piccata (thin escalope) of veal in a mildly
    spicy cream sauce
Cheese: semi-matured Soumaintrain with
    apricot halves

Other wines to go with this dish
Chablis Grand Cru
Chassagne Montrachet
Pessac-Léognan Blanc
Alsace-Riesling Grand Cru
Brut Vintage Blanc de Blancs Champagne
Hawke's Bay Chardonnay (New-Zealand,
    around 5 years old)

The sommelier's selection
Domaine Bonneau du Martray
Domaine Chevalier
Domaine du Pavillon
Domaine Michel Juillot

CHAMPAGNE BLANC BRUT
scallops with white butter sauce

AOC
Champagne
REGION
Champagne
DRY WHITE
SPARKLING WINE
**This AOC also
produces
moelleux
effervescent
whites and rosés**
AREA
31,000ha
CULTIVARS
**Chardonnay
(the only cultivar
in a Blanc de
Blancs
Champagne)
Pinot Noir
Pinot Meunier**

I love the refinement of Champagne with this kind of dish, that jostling of delicate bubbles against the dense flesh of the barely seared scallops, with the silky sauce offsetting the gassy acidity of the sparkling wine.

Personally, I tend to prefer Champagne as an aperitif. But as I know from my experience as a sommelier, there are plenty of meals that you can plan around Champagne because it goes well with a wide range of dishes. One thing I cannot stand however is seeing a delicious Champagne wasted on an unsuitable dessert. If you like to finish a meal with Champagne, serve it long enough after the coffee to become fully receptive to those delicate Champagne aromas.

A Brut Champagne with scallops in white butter sauce offers refinement at every level. First, there is the alliance of textures: the fleshy mollusc (crispy on the outside, moist on the inside) and the cushiony, sparkling wine. Then there is the taste – the iodised aromas in the scallop, with its taste of the sea, blending with the mineral notes in the Champagne, with its taste of a limestone terroir. Serving a Brut Champagne Blanc de Blancs (exclusively made from the Chardonnay grape) means that you can also serve the wine as the aperitif – useful because the scallops have to be cooked at the very last moment. Chill the Champagne to 8°C (46.4°F), taste it before the meal and then leave it to warm slightly in the glasses. That way, it will have warmed to a temperature of 11°C (51.8°F) by the time the scallops are ready. A Champagne at this temperature plays on its velvetiness and lends itself to a variety of combinations. I recently tasted a 10 year old vintage Champagne with saucisson (dry sausage) and pistachios in puff pastry. Not an obvious match by any means, but an entirely successful one as it turned out.

For best results when cooling the Champagne, instead of an ice bucket (which tends to over-chill the wine) use a bucket of water containing just a few ice cubes.

Other dishes to go with this wine
A vintage Blanc de Noirs is generally a better choice than a Blanc de Blancs when planning an entire meal around one Champagne.
Lobster or crayfish in aromatic broth
Crispy baked bass and red mullet with
    foie gras and tomato coulis
Fillets of sole or turbot in a
    Champagne sauce
Bresse chicken in a cream sauce
Mallard fillets marinated in Champagne
Langres, semi-dry goat's cheese or
    Chaource, avoiding any ash-coated
    goat's cheese

Other wines to go with this dish
    Effervescent wines:
The Crémants de Loire, Alsace, Burgundy
    or the Limoux
    Still wines:
Savennières Sec
Vouvray Sec
Alsace Pinot Blanc
Mosel-Saar-Ruwer (Germany)

The sommelier's selection
Veuve Clicquot-Ponsardin,
Duval-Leroy, Gratien,
Jacquesson, Lanson,
Laurent-Perrier,
Moët et Chandon,
Pol Roger, Pommery,
Roederer, Ruinart,
Salon, Selosse

COTEAUX DU LANGUEDOC BLANC
warm salt cod brandade

AOC
Coteaux du Languedoc
REGION
Languedoc
WHITE WINE
This AOC also produces 75% reds and 13% rosés
AREA
1,200ha given to whites (total 10,000ha)
CULTIVARS
Clairette
Grenache Blanc
Bourboulenc
Piquepoul
Marsanne
Roussanne

This is a great Mediterranean classic with all the fragrance of the Midi: smooth creamy texture, usually with a hint of garlic, and a natural affinity for full-bodied, generous wines.

Cod brandade is popular throughout the Midi from Provence to the Languedoc. It is traditionally made with poached desalted cod, puréed with olive oil and reduced to a thick, creamy consistency. It is more or less seasoned with garlic, depending on the recipe and the region of origin, and may be eaten cold or warm. Personally I like it warm, on toast as an appetizer. The Languedoc winegrower who first introduced me to this version of brandade naturally served it with a white Languedoc wine – a winning combination to my mind, with bags of personality.

Brandade is quite salty, creamy on the palate despite its somewhat stringy texture, and ideally suited to a smooth, almost lush white wine. Overly wooded wines are best avoided, especially if the dish makes sparing use of garlic. All things considered, what springs to mind is a youngish (two years old) Côteaux du Languedoc Blanc from a reputable winegrower. When properly made, these wines offer density and alcoholic strength coupled with a nose of white-fleshed fruit (peaches and pears) and the aniseed notes of the Grenache – all in all, quite enough texture to stand up to a brandade. The problem with this sort of combination is that it all depends on the kind of wine and the kind of brandade – because the wines do vary enormously across the appellation. A more strongly wooded, more Provençal style of wine, for instance – such as a self-assured Palette Blanc - would be a better match for a pungently garlicky, typically Provençal brandade. A cold brandade on the other hand would go best with a regional wine that made more of the mineral element - a Picpoul-de-Pinet, for instance. The fact is that nothing is simple when it comes to brandade - so in the end, how you eat it and what wine you choose to eat it with are largely up to you.

Other wines to go with this dish
White wines:
Bandol
Châteauneuf-du-Pape
Patrimonio
Nuragus di Cagliari (Sardinia, Italy)
Vino Cinque Terra (Liguria, Italy)
Red wines:
Vin de Pays d'Oc Merlot
Oltrepo Pavese (Italy)
Merlot du Tessin (Switzerland)

Other dishes to go with this wine
Grilled sardines or marinade of sardines
Fried calamari
Stuffed baby squid
Platter of Cévennes saucisson
    and green olives
Cod steak in a white sauce
Mackerel in white wine, with gherkins
    and coriander
Peppers stuffed with brandade
Cauliflower au gratin
Salad of Larzac Chèvre Frais (cheese)

The sommelier's selection
Château l'Hospitalet
Château Puech-Haut
Domaine Les Aurelles
Domaine Saint-Jean de Bebian

TURSAN BLANC
pibale (young eels)

AOVDQS
Tursan
REGION
South West France
WHITE WINE
This AOC also produces reds and rosés
AREA
160ha given to whites (total 460ha)
CULTIVARS
Mainly: Baroque Also: Sauvignon Gros Manseng

This disappearing but deliciously delicate dish consists of young eels with a sprinkling of Espelette peppers. The wine to go with it must not interfere with the subtle fish flavours, yet be strong enough to stand up to the peppers.

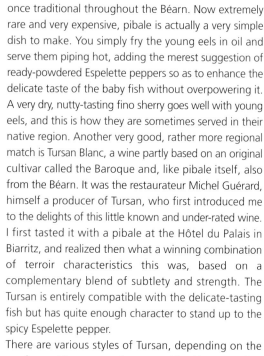

Pibale is a dish from the South West of France that was once traditional throughout the Béarn. Now extremely rare and very expensive, pibale is actually a very simple dish to make. You simply fry the young eels in oil and serve them piping hot, adding the merest suggestion of ready-powdered Espelette peppers so as to enhance the delicate taste of the baby fish without overpowering it. A very dry, nutty-tasting fino sherry goes well with young eels, and this is how they are sometimes served in their native region. Another very good, rather more regional match is Tursan Blanc, a wine partly based on an original cultivar called the Baroque and, like pibale itself, also from the Béarn. It was the restaurateur Michel Guérard, himself a producer of Tursan, who first introduced me to the delights of this little known and under-rated wine. I first tasted it with a pibale at the Hôtel du Palais in Biarritz, and realized then what a winning combination of terroir characteristics this was, based on a complementary blend of subtlety and strength. The Tursan is entirely compatible with the delicate-tasting fish but has quite enough character to stand up to the spicy Espelette pepper.

There are various styles of Tursan, depending on the producer. My own preference with this somewhat contrasting dish is a fairly wooded wine with lightly oxidized aromas, intense freshness and a sumptuous nose revealing notes of pears, apples and citrus. These characteristics add even greater boldness. At the same time – and this is the Tursan's strongest point – it has a delightfully fanciful side that strikes an almost noble cord with the pibale.

Other wines to go with this dish
Irouléguy Blanc (4-5 years old)
Fino Sherry (Spain)
Lightly wooded vintage Champagne (8-10 years old)
Not too wooded crianza-style Rueda Blanco (Spain)

Other dishes to go with this wine
Canapés of fish tartar with herbs and lemon, as an appetizer
Freshwater fish, deglazed with lemon
Poultry breast pan-fried with slow-cooked turnips
Cheeses: Tomme des Pyrénées, Rocamadour

The sommelier's selection
Château de Bachen
Château de Perchade
Les Vignerons de Tursan

HERMITAGE BLANC
pikeperch with star anise and bamboo shoots

AOC
Hermitage
REGION
Rhône Valley
WHITE WINE
**This AOC also
produces
80% reds and
a few whites
vinified as Vins
de Paille**
AREA
**25ha given to
whites (total
125ha)**
CULTIVARS
**Marsanne
Roussanne**

This magnificently contrasting dish sets the smooth flesh of the freshwater fish against the pungently floral aromas of the star anise and the crisp yet velvety texture of the bamboo shoots. The challenge is to create a harmony with a wine that plays on this complexity.

Pikeperch is a delicately flavoured, white-fleshed fish that is easily overcooked. It is best oven baked, in a covered dish so as to preserve all of its lovely firm texture. Make the sauce separately using white wine and fish stock lightly infused with star anise to add a mild but not over-powering aniseed flavour. The bamboo shoots will add extra crispness.

The wine will have to measure up on several levels: texture, aroma and, most important of all, freshness. The first place I ever tasted a Hermitage Blanc with pikeperch and star anise was Tain-L'Hermitage itself when I went there several years ago to judge a sommelier contest. I have always liked the Rhône Valley wines and Hermitage, with its density and sense of contrast, is very much one of them. The generosity of the sunny Roussanne grape is nicely coupled with the freshness of the Marsanne and the austerity of northern wines. I love its caressing roundness and precise structure, hint of acidity and expansive tannins. I love its mineral taste of terroir and gorgeous nose dominated by notes of honey, beeswax and acacia – so perfectly in tune with aniseed and liquorice. For this dish, be sure to choose an Hermitage that has aged for 10 years or so, decant it to bring out its fullness and serve it at 11-12°C (51.8-53.6°F). It will go beautifully with the pikeperch and star anise, creating a match of exceptional elegance that balances sensuality and rigor, mineral edge and roundness, suaveness and precision.

Other dishes to go with this wine
Poultry terrine with hazelnuts, almonds
    or pistachios
Crab terrine
Medallion of lobster Bellevue, mayonnaise
Roasted saffron lobster
Spiny lobster American-style
Pikeperch or pike quenelles with white
    sauce or Nantua-style sauce
Turkey breast with foie gras and
    Dauphiné-style potatoes au gratin
Veal escalope with cream and mushrooms
Blanquette de veau (veal stew
    old-fashioned style) with white rice
Salsify stuffed with truffles au gratin
Saint-Marcellin or Picodon cheese

With an Hermitage Vin de Paille
Iced bombe flavoured with star anise

Other wines to go with this dish
Châteauneuf-du-Pape Blanc
Pessac-Léognan Blanc (7-10 years old)

The sommelier's selection
Cave de Tain
Domaine Ferraton
Domaine Marc Sorrel
Domaine Jean-Louis Chave
Maison Paul Jaboulet aÎné

MACON BLANC

trout with almonds

AOC
Mâcon
REGION
Burgundy
WHITE WINE
**This AOC also
produces
75% reds**
AREA
**800ha given to
whites (total
3,500ha)**
CULTIVAR
Chardonnay

Trout with almonds may be classical, but the different textures of the delicately fleshed fish, buttery sauce and roasted almonds make this a difficult dish to combine with wine.

This dish always makes me think of the freshly fished mountain trout my grandmother used to serve at her restaurant in Briançon. Fond memories of a now old-fashioned dish that is thankfully still served in a few traditional restaurants. Choosing a wine to go with it is not easy due to the variety of textures and tastes that must be taken into account. There is the flaky flesh of the trout, the sauce (which can be very rich) and the toasted almond garnish bathing in butter. What you need with a dish like this is a rounded, generous and persistent wine. Great classic though it is, this is all the same a very simple dish, so you should choose a good but well-priced wine. A Mâcon, from one of the Burgundy rising stars, will fit the bill here. It is made from the Chardonnay grape, like most of the Burgundy whites, and varies widely in style depending on the area of production. I am particularly fond of the Viré et Clessé Mâcon wines. With their good balance of mineral crispness and generosity, evolving toward warm notes of nuts and Viennese pastry, there can be no better, more complementary match for our trout. A three year old Mâcon served at 8-9°C (46.4-48.2°F) will bring a welcome freshness that balances the richness of the dish, while its straightforward, sometimes austere roundness will never interfere with the delicate succulence of the fish.

Other dishes to go with this wine
Charcuterie appetizer
White sausage
Cervelle de Canut (a herbed cream cheese
    from Lyon, served on toast)
Back of cod with sea salt
Seafood pot-au-feu
Lyon saucisson in brioche
Andouillette in mustard sauce
Cheese: Chèvres du Mâconnais,
    Chavignol Demi-Sec, Boutons de Culotte

Other wines to go with this dish
Alsace Pinot Gris
Beaujolais Blanc
Saint-Joseph Blanc
Côtes du Jura Blanc
Chinon Blanc
Friuli Chardonnay (Italy)
Chardonnay, Maipo Valley (Chile)

The sommelier's selection
Domaine Bonhomme
Domaine Guffens-Heynen
Domaine Valette
Domaine Les Hauts d'Azenay
Domaine Thévenet

QUINCY

salmon with sorrel

AOC
Quincy
REGION
Loire
WHITE WINE
AREA
180ha
CULTIVAR
Sauvignon

This recipe created by the Troisgros family in the '80s has since become a seminal favourite. The acidity of the herb, tempered by the discreet presence of the cream, marries well with the fondant flesh of the salmon.

Salmon with sorrel sauce is a feast for the eyes. The salmon should be cooked on one side only as recommended by Pierre Troisgros, so preserving all of its lovely pink colour that shows through the sorrel green tones of the sauce coating. This contrast of colours is echoed by the complementary flavours of the naturally oily fish set against the bitter tones of the sorrel. The green acidity of the sorrel, softened but not overpowered by the cream, is what determines our choice of wine: white, crisp and straightforward with plenty of fruit and roundness. A Chardonnay would be quite unsuitable in this case because the extreme finesse of the wine would strike a very discordant note with the strident sorrel. To my mind, the best partner for our sorrel-flavoured salmon would be a Sauvignon-based Quincy, one of the Loire wines. It originates from the siliceous soils along the borders of the Sologne, and displays a personality that is fairly unique among Sauvignon wines. With its rounded, generous and easily approachable style, a Quincy is always expressive but never obtrusive. It is an obvious match for the salmon that was traditionally fished in the Loire; and it's sharp, crisply mineral but not biting freshness makes it a perfect foil for the sorrel. The beauty of this combination is its crystalline harmony. I first tasted it in a restaurant on the Sologne River and, then as now, I am always struck by the tranquil elegance of this match – a now-famous dish in partnership with a wine from a little-known appellation that is well worth getting to know.

Other wines to go with this dish
Menetou-Salon
Reuilly
Touraine Sauvignon
Graves Blanc
Sainte-Foy-Bordeaux Blanc
Premières Côtes de Blaye Blanc

Other dishes to go with this wine
Rabbit terrine with herbs
Mousse of freshwater fish with
  shredded carrots
Charcuterie: saucisson, cured country
  ham and andouille (not over-smoky)
Small frogs legs, breaded and fried with
  chopped parsley and garlic
Brill with sorrel
Grilled Mediterranean bass or
  gilt-head bream

The sommelier's selection
Domaine Jacques Sallé
Domaine du Tremblay
Domaine Sorbe
Domaine Trotereau

CHATEAUNEUF-DU-PAPE BLANC
bay-leaf flavoured John Dory with courgettes

AOC
Châteauneuf-du-Pape
REGION
Rhône Valley
WHITE WINE
This AOC also produces 95% reds
AREA
200ha given to whites (total 3,200ha)
CULTIVARS
**Mainly:
Roussanne
Marsanne
Also:
Grenache Blanc
Clairette
Piquepoul
Picardan
Bourboulenc**

I love the harmony of sea and earth tastes in this dish. The wine to go with it must be particularly subtle so as to match the bay leaf aromas without interfering with the firm, fleshy taste of the fish.

There is something unmistakably Mediterranean about a John Dory cooked with bay leaves. But take care, when slipping the bay leaves under the skin of the fish prior to cooking, that you do not kill the delicate flavour of the white-fleshed fish. As it cooks, the fish becomes lightly infused with herby aromas that are then highlighted by a drizzle of olive oil and a sprinkling of sea salt immediately before serving. The courgettes are simply pan-fried in olive oil with a touch of garlic. Their rather soft texture can be a problem when it comes to choosing a wine, but otherwise this is an intensely tasty dish that calls for a wine from the same terroir. The combination of firm-fleshed fish, bay leaf, garlic and olive oil needs a generous, even lively wine with a good blend of intensity and freshness.

For me, John Dory with bay leaves will always carry very special connotations because it's one of the dishes that I had to match with a wine when I entered the World's Best Sommelier Competition in Rio in 1992. What sprang to mind that day, because it seemed the obvious choice, was a white Châteauneuf-du-Pape. The appellation is of course famous for its great red wines but the whites, produced in smaller quantities, go better with Mediterranean cuisine. Those I prefer are around five years old with aromas of spring flowers and white-fleshed fruits from the Rhône Valley (pears, peaches) and just the merest suggestion of aniseed. Warm but not too warm on the palate, they combine a lovely fullness with a good clean attack. Their strength works wonders with the John Dory, while their discreet garrigue-like aromas echo the herby fragrance of the bay leaf. The finish leaves the mouth on a sensation of thirst-quenching crispness punctuated by a distinct hint of green almonds.

Other wines to go with this dish
Palette Blanc
Côteaux du Languedoc Blanc
Pessac-Léognan Blanc
Meursault
Puligny
Penedes Blanco (Spain)
Carneros Chardonnay (USA)

Other dishes to go with this wine
Terrine of Mediterranean fish
Grilled gilt-head bream or red sea bream
Bass with fennel
Tuna carpaccio with olive oil and white
   asparagus tips
Picodon cheese

The sommelier's selection
Château Mont Redon
Clos du Mont Olivet
Domaine de Beaurenard
Domaine de Nalys
Domaine Marchand

PATRIMONIO BLANC
grilled turbot with fennel

AOC
Patrimonio
REGION
Corsica
WHITE WINE
**This AOC also
produces
50% reds and
35% rosés**
AREA
**60ha given
to whites
(total 400ha)**
CULTIVAR
Vermentino

Broiled turbot takes on a dense, succulent texture, with smoky aromas that intensify the strongly aniseed tones of the slow-cooked fennel garnish.

The noble turbot is renowned for its firm, tasty flesh, but it does need careful cooking. It will lose all of its delicacy if overdone. Here it is served with a garnish of pulped slow-cooked fennel bulbs, a combination that adds to the elegance of the fish and conjures up irresistible images of warm Mediterranean summers.

What I love about this dish is the contrast between the almost al dente texture of the grilled fish and the softness of the aniseed-flavoured vegetable. It is easily matched with a wine, focusing on a theme of velvety smoothness so as to create a seamless combination of flavours. For a harmony of this sort, a white Patrimonio wine fits the bill perfectly. Patrimonio is Corsica's star appellation. It combines the generosity of grapes ripened under a southern sun with just enough mineral fabric for good crispness. Freshness is particularly important on the finish when the strong taste of the fennel could so easily overpower the other flavours. After a full attack, the Patrimonio develops fresh notes of citronella that marry deliciously with the taste of the turbot. But what I especially love is the unpretentious elegance of this combination, based on such natural, healthy products.

Other wines to go with this dish
Châteauneuf-du-Pape Blanc
Côteaux du Languedoc Blanc
Côteaux Varois Blanc
Costières de Nîmes Blanc
Alsace Riesling
Chinon Blanc
Penedes Blanco (Spain)
Corvo di Casteldaccia (Sicily, Italy)

Other dishes to go with this wine
Corsican Brocciu (soft sheep's cheese) terrine
Cold oysters in watercress aspic
Bass with fennel and Pastis sauce
Spaghetti with seafood
Rolled cured ham with tapenade
  and dried tomatoes
Fresh goat's or sheep's cheese

The sommelier's selection
Domaine Arena
Domaine de Catarelli
Domaine Giudicelli
Domaine Leccia

MEURSAULT BLANC
crispy bass in a potato millefeuille topped with foie gras

AOC
Meursault
REGION
Burgundy
WHITE WINE
**This AOC also
produces
5% reds**
AREA
**360ha given
to whites
(total 375ha)**
CULTIVAR
Chardonnay

This delicately constructed millefeuille consists of layers of grated potato cakes alternating with slices of firm-fleshed bass then topped with a sliver of foie gras. The wine must handle the complexity of the dish without making it seem bland.

The elegant, flavoursome bass is ideally suited to delicate cuisine such as this complex millefeuille with its layers of pan-fried fish and starchy potatoes plus a velvety topping of foie gras. A tomato coulis softened by just a dash of cream adds the final touch to a list of ingredients guaranteed to make any gourmet go weak at the knees. This much sought-after concoction is the brainchild of leading chef André Lallican at the Bistrot du Sommelier in Paris. Serving this millefeuille is a task in itself since the ingredients must be assembled at the very last minute. The taste is strikingly voluminous: a seamless blend of earth and sea flavours that preserves the subtle taste of the bass despite the cushiony presence of the foie gras and potatoes. Last of all, there is that refreshing touch of tomato coulis, an ingredient essential to the recipe but likely to cause even more problems when it comes to choosing the wine – which is already not an easy choice.

Having tried various combinations, I decided in the end that the only wine capable of doing justice to the complexity of this dish was a Meursault, one of the most celebrated Burgundy whites. Generous and smooth but with plenty of spirit, it also has a clean mineral tang that avoids any hint of blandness. To my mind, what goes best with bass and foie gras is a mature Meursault, (6-7 years old) served at 12°C (53.6°F) so as to bring out its full force. It should be long on the palate, delicately wooded, full-bodied and intense, providing the perfect soul mate for our bass. This is a marriage based more on softness than contrast, one in which the bass and foie gras seem to combine with the Meursault in what I would call a 'spherical union'.

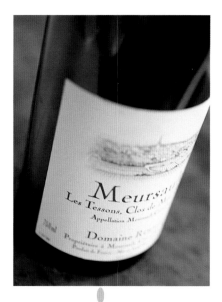

Other wines to go with this dish
Mâçon Blanc (preferably from the
    Viré-Clessé sector)
Palette Blanc
Châteauneuf-du-Pape Blanc
Graves Blanc
Alsace Riesling Vendanges Tardives
    (around 10 years old)
Sonoma County Chardonnay
    (California, USA)
Barossa Valley Chardonnay (S Australia)

Other dishes to go with this wine
Lobster in aromatic broth
Spiny lobster or king prawns roasted in
    their juice with spices
Poultry or fish quenelles in sauce
White sausage with truffles
Bresse chicken with cream
Blanquette de veau old-fashioned style
    with white rice
Seafood risotto
Dauphiné-style potatoes au gratin
Courgettes au gratin with rice

The sommelier's selection
Domaine Coche Dury
Domaine des Comtes Lafon
Domaine Roulot
Domaine Morey Pierre
Domaine Jean-Marc Boillot
Maison Bouchard Père et Fils
Domaine Jacques Prieur

COSTIERES DE NIMES ROUGE
red mullet with tapenade

AOC
Costières de
Nîmes
REGION
Languedoc
RED WINE
This AOC also
produces
20% rosés and
5% whites
AREA
2,800ha given
to reds (total
3,500ha)
CULTIVARS
Mainly:
Syrah
Grenache
Mourvèdre
Also:
Cinsault
Carignan

This somewhat gamy-tasting fish of the rocks goes best with red wine – particularly when served as here with a Provençal tapenade (puréed capers, pitted black olives, anchovy and herbs with olive oil and lemon juice).

I am often asked about fish with red wine, particularly when one wine is to be served throughout the meal. A fish like red mullet simplifies things considerably because its tight-textured, intensely tasty flesh happens to go very well with red wine – as does as its colour. A particularly good combination is this dish of small red mullet, cooked ungutted (so as to preserve the delicate tasting liver) then garnished with a scoop of black olive tapenade and Camargue rice prepared with pearl onions and lardons. The garnish is very much a feature of this distinctive combination and must be sufficiently discreet so as to avoid overloading the palate with too many flavours.

When it comes to choosing and serving the wine, there are a few points to bear in mind. Firstly, steer well clear of overly vegetal reds (such as those based on the Cabernet Franc). Likewise avoid any that are too wooded or, in particular, too tannic. Your best bet is a Syrah-based or failing that a Merlot-based red. Personally, I think a Costières de Nîmes makes a very good match for red mullet. This is a dense, well-structured wine from an area halfway between the River Rhône and the Languedoc. Choose a 3-4 year old wine, served fairly cool (around 15°C/59°F) so that the alcohol does not become unpleasantly over-powering, spoiling the taste of the fish. The combination of sensations here is actually quite complex: the suppleness of the Costières de Nîmes, set against the persistency of the fish flavours, while the discreet tapenade garnish echoes that suggestion of black olives in the wine.

Other dishes to go with this wine
Lamb pie with chard ribs
Aubergine caviar
Grilled top rump or entrecote of beef
Duck in cocotte with onions and lardons
Ratatouille Nice-style
Warm Pélardon cheese with toast
   and tapenade
Cheeses: Tomme de Savoie or Tomme des
   Pyrénées, Saint-Nectaire
Red berry ice-cream
Cherry batter pudding

Other wines to go with this dish
Côteaux Varois Red
Bellet Rouge
Palette Rouge
Graves Rouge
Stellenbosch Syrah (South Africa)
Alexander Valley Merlot
   (California, USA)

The sommelier's selection
Château Bolchet
Château de Campuget
Château de l'Amarine
Château la Tuilerie
Château Mas Neuf des Costières
Château Mourgues du Grès

PESSAC-LEOGNAN ROUGE

lampreys bordeaux-style with slow-cooked leeks

AOC
Pessac-Léognan
REGION
Bordeaux
RED WINE
This AOC also produces 20% whites
AREA
1,000ha given to reds (total 1,300ha)
CULTIVARS
**Mainly:
Cabernet-Sauvignon
Cabernet-Franc
Merlot
Also:
Carmenère
Malbec
Petit Verdot**

Freshwater fish in a red wine sauce with slow-cooked leeks leeks is one of the finest examples of Gironde cuisine. It marries beautifully with the great red wines of the Graves region.

Lampreys, strictly speaking, are not fish but aquatic vertebrates whose flesh retains a salty quality despite their freshwater habitat. Their decidedly fishy flavour makes the choice of red wine quite difficult and rules out a dry white wine altogether. Anything too tannic, too heady or too gorged with sun would be distinctly out of balance with such typically regional fare. What does go well with this dish however, despite that hint of pungency from the leeks, is a Graves from the Pessac area. The overall effect is as surprising as it is successful, relying as it does on the mineral fruitiness of the wine to bring out a matching quality in the sauce. A Pessac-Léognan is a very elegant wine with all the smoothness required to go with fish. I love its light, fruity, distinctively terroir style and the way it adapts to such a wide range of dishes, including some far more exotic than lampreys. It goes admirably well with beef teppanyaki, for instance, a Japanese dish of stir-fried meat cooked and eaten off a teppan griddle. A Pessac-Léognan is an ideal choice when only one wine is to be served throughout the meal.

This is a thoroughbred of a wine, with a rich black-fruit nose and fine silky tannins that marry beautifully with tender meats. With lampreys, I prefer a fairly young Pessac-Léognan, served at around 15-16°C (59-60.8°F). Cooling the wine helps to bring out its fresh, mineral qualities, making a subtle foil for the velvety smoothness of the sauce.

Other dishes to go with this wine
Pikeperch with red butter
Grilled gilt-head bream with thyme
　and rosemary
Roast chicken with garlic in its skin
　and pan-fried mushrooms
Entrecôte Bordeaux style
Red berry soup with blackcurrant ice-cream
Blackcurrant granita (granular sorbet)
Miroir au cassis (blackcurrant caramel)

Other wines to go with this dish
Graves Rouge
Margaux
Sancerre Rouge
Reuilly Rouge
Sainte-Foy-Bordeaux Rouge

The sommelier's selection
Château de France
Château Haut-Bailly
Château Haut-Bergey
Château Haut-Brion
Château Malartic-Lagravière
Château La Louvière
Château Pape Clément

PECHARMANT

salmis of guinea fowl with white kidney beans

AOC
Pécharmant
REGION
**South West
France**
RED WINE
AREA
400ha
CULTIVARS
**Merlot
Cabernet Franc
Cabernet-
Sauvignon
Côt**

This combination of meat, stuffing and kidney beans is traditional throughout South West France – sliced, boned and rolled guinea fowl, stuffed with giblets and herbs and served with the juice of the pressed carcass. It plays on a variety of textures and intense flavours that the wine must balance.

The smell of herb stuffing fills the air as the piping-hot guinea fowl is brought to the table. Aromas of parsley, chives and estragon seem to vie for supremacy. The meat itself has a wonderful delicacy, with the succulence of the minced giblets set against the firm-fleshed guinea fowl basted in its juices, the whole impression nicely balanced by the soft-centred, thin-skinned kidney beans. You need just the right blend of seasonings for a salmis, preferably using a delicately musky pepper such as Cameroon pepper that will bring out the range of aromas without overpowering them.

When it comes to choosing the wine, the riot of aroma and texture in this dish is a real problem. What you do not want is a wine that might seem too fluid or delicate by comparison. We need an honest, well-structured red – one with a good chewy texture that gives you a balance of strength and density. For a classically regional match, I can think of no better wine than the richly coloured Pécharmant from South West France. This a wine that can seem a bit austere in its youth but it softens up nicely with 5-7 years aging, releasing aromas of black-skinned fruits, violets, smoke, leather and flint. The tannins will hold out well against the rather rich salmis stuffing and the overall structure of the wine will easily survive the starchiness of the kidney beans. But a Pécharmant is not just a robust wine. It also has a deeply mineral side that adds an extra touch of refinement to this match. The wine is usually all the better for decanting an hour before serving, growing more expressive and elegant but remaining every bit as forthright.

Other dishes to go with this wine
Poultry liver or game terrine
Salad of potted gizzards
Duck breast fillet with blackcurrants
Potted duck
Cassoulet
Hanger steak with shallots
Pot-au-feu
Beef stew
Beef on a string
Potatoes au gratin
Pan-fried mushrooms, ceps with cream
Sheep's cheese (Tomme de brebis des Pyrénées)
Blue cheese (Fourme d'Ambert,
   Bleu de Bresse)

Other wines to go with this this dish
Madiran
Cahors
Irouléguy Rouge
Cornas
Gigondas Rouge
Bandol Rouge
Rioja (Spain)
Malbec/Tannat-based wines from
   Mendoza Province (Argentina)

The sommelier's selection
Château de Biran
Château de Tiregand
Château La Tilleraie
Domaine du Haut-Pécharmant

ALSACE PINOT NOIR ROUGE
quail with grapes

AOC
Alsace Pinot Noir
REGION
Alsace
RED WINE
**This AOC also
produces rosés**
AREA
1,225ha
CULTIVAR
Pinot Noir

I like to serve this dish in the fall when grapes are in season. The grapes should be black if possible, not overly acid and only added to the dish after the quail has finished roasting. This conserves the meat's freshness and lightness – which must be complemented by the choice of wine.

The succulent, discreetly fragrant flesh of the refined, gourmet quail can easily be overcooked. To conserve its finesse, it is best roasted in its own juices, with just the barest touch of seasoning. An overly powerful wine is out of the question with such a delicate bird. Only a very light wine can do justice to its subtle aromas and tight-textured flesh.

I first tasted this quintessentially French dish with an Alsace Pinot Noir toward the end of the 1970s while I was staying in Colmar with my father – it was striking to see how well wine and quail went together. Alsace Pinot Noir is an exception in a region that is otherwise devoted to white-wine production. But it can be really first-rate in a good year when the grapes have ripened to perfection: lovely vibrant red colour, distinctly raspberry nose (in the young wines) and mineral characteristics as diverse as the soils of Alsace. To my mind, a young, delicately wooded Pinot Noir works wonders with quail and grapes. The fluid limpidity of the wine matches the subtlety of the bird while its light grapey acidity echoes the fruitiness of the garnish. Serving the wine at a respectable 16°C (60.8°F) adds to the harmony by enhancing the freshness of the grapes.

Other dishes to go with this wine
    With a 2-4 year old wine:
Poultry terrine with toast
Snail pot with garlic
Grilled red mullet
Pan-fried veal liver with
    raspberry vinegar
Brie or Coulommiers cheese
Raspberries in fruit soup
    With a 5-7 year old wine:
Sautéed mushrooms, garlic and parsley
Woodpigeon/woodcock in its juice
Escalope Milanese-style with fresh pasta
Grilled rib of beef

Other wines to go with this dish
Mercurey Rouge
Mâcon Rouge
Menetou-Salon Rouge
Bugey Rouge
Rioja Tinto Crianza (Spain)

The sommelier's selection
Domaine du Clos Saint-Landelin
Domaine Marcel Deiss
Maison Hugel

VOSNE-ROMANEE

bresse chicken with st george's mushrooms

The star of this noble combination has to be the Vosne-Romanée – because anyone lucky enough to serve such a rare and precious wine should know how to do it justice.

A Vosne-Romanée is one of the majestic reds from the Côte de Nuits. Its area of appellation is famed for such legendary Grands Crus as Romanée-Conti, La Romanée, Romanée Saint-Vivant, La Tâche and Richebourg, together with superb if slightly less rare Premiers Crus (Les Beaux Monts and Les Malconsorts). A Vosne-Romanée has that near perfection that invites superlatives. It is everything a wine should be and more besides: refined, elegant, powerful, full-bodied, dense, long on the palate and infinitely velvety. Wasting it, should you be lucky enough to have a bottle, would be nothing short of criminal. Patience is the first rule with a Vosne-Romanée: this is a wine that will keep you waiting for at least five years. When the time does come to open it, the wine should be served at 17-18°C (62.6 -64.4°F) and allowed to air in the glass rather than the decanter (because you don't want to lose those spicy, almost eastern notes). With a plump Bresse chicken, what strikes you first are the complementary textures of the crispy-skinned roasted poultry and the smooth, silky wine. Then there is the explosion of fragrance on the nose and palate: roasted notes on the plate and in the glass, plus those blackcurrant and raspberry aromas typical of the great Burgundies. In a more mature Vosne-Romanée, the fruit evolves from these primary scents toward a stunning complexity of violets and the forest floor in the autumn. This is where the St George's mushrooms come in, echoing the tertiary notes in the wine with an infusion of flavours that make up in balance what they lack in texture. Tender flesh, crispy skin, velvety wine, scented wood mushrooms: the play of contrasting and complementary sensations creates an impression of memorable harmony.

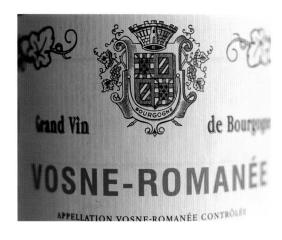

Other wines to go with this dish
Red wines:
Nuits-Saints-Georges
Vougeot
Saint-Julien
Margaux
    White wines:
Meursault
Chablis Grand Cru
Hermitage
Côtes du Jura

Other dishes to go with this wine
Pheasant terrine
Duck with turnips
Venison fillet with brown sauce
Beef fillet with mushroom
Veal medallions with soft spices

The sommelier's selection
Domaine Faiveley
Domaine Anne Gros
Domaine des Perdrix
Domaine Jayer Henri
Domaine Leroy
Domaine Méo-Camuzet
Domaine Mongeard-Mugneret
Maison Dominique Laurent

SAVENNIERES
chicken pot-au-feu

AOC
Savennières
REGION
Loire
WHITE WINE
Dry or Moelleux
AREA
Approx 20ha for
Savennières
Coulée-de-
Serrant
(total 135ha)
CULTIVAR
Chenin

Rather like a boiled fowl, a chicken pot-au-feu owes its delicate bouquet to the variety of vegetables infused in the clove-steeped broth. The wine to go with it – white or a light red – must show the same discretion.

The quality of ingredients in this recipe is quite as important as the way you prepare them. The chicken in particular – which can also be a hen – should not be overcooked. It should remain somewhat firm so as to complement the variety of textures and flavours in the spring vegetables: carrots, turnips, potatoes, celery, leeks and onions. Simmering these in the chicken broth infuses them with the flavours of the herbs included as seasoning (thyme, bay leaf and clove-stuck onion). At the end of cooking, the broth is reduced and thickened with a dash of cream, and used as the sauce for the velvety chicken and vegetables.

To my mind, this simple, almost humble dish definitely goes better with a white wine, and a Chenin-based Savennières white in particular. The Savennières vineyard is one of the first Loire Valley vineyards I ever visited as a sommelier, and to this day I retain a special fondness for its dry but never sharp white wines. I love their almost tender character with those typical terroir notes of schist and sandstone. Served at 11°C (51°F), a Savennières Blanc Sec releases aromas of orchard fruits, citrus and springtime notes, plus the occasional hint of verbena. There is a natural and gentle harmony with the chicken pot-au-feu, thanks to the smoothness and aromatic diversity of the wine – and that hint of acidity on the finish avoids any trace of blandness.

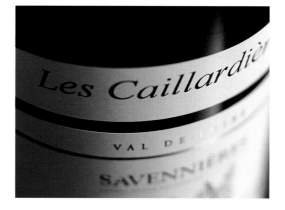

Other wines to go with this dish
White wines:
Alsace Riesling
Anjou
Vouvray Sec
Montlouis Sec
Jurançon Sec
Stellenbosch Sauvignon (South Africa)
Paarl Chenin Blanc (South Africa)
Malborough Sauvignon (New Zealand)
Red wines (tender):
Gamay de Touraine
Beaujolais
Côtes du Rhône (young)
Merlot du Tessin (Switzerland)

Other dishes to go with this wine
Peeled shrimps with lemon as an appetizer
Asparagus in a fine mousse sauce
Pan-fried scallops with sea salt and
    pink peppercorns on a bed of leeks
Pikeperch or pike with white butter
Shad with white butter
Roasted andouille de Guéméné* with
    stewed apples and white wine sauce
Cauliflower, christophines and sweet
    potatoes au gratin
Ash-coated goat's cheese: Pyramide de
    Valençay, Sainte-Maure
Cooked pears with vanilla ice-cream
Baked apple with vanilla ice-cream
*A type of chitterling sausage

The sommelier's selection
Château d'Épire
Coulée de Serrant
Domaine du Closel
Domaine Pierre Soulez

CHAMBOLLE-MUSIGNY
duckling with braised turnips

AOC
Chambolle-Musigny
REGION
Burgundy
RED WINE
AREA
60ha given to the Chambolle-Musigny Premier Cru (total 210ha)
CULTIVAR
Pinot Noir

Duck, irrespective of the recipe, is always a challenge when it comes to choosing the wine because its intensely tasty flesh will tend to eclipse the other flavours.

It's never easy combining duck with wine. Basically, you have a choice of two approaches. Either you can step up the volume, choosing a dense, very intense and structured wine that will hold out nicely against the powerful duck. Or you can aim for a balance of complementary qualities, creating a match based on finesse and elegance. The slow cooking time of this particular recipe simplifies things a bit because it softens the taste of the turnips and gives the meat an almost potted consistency. It also concentrates the overall bouquet. To my mind, that calls for a complex, naturally elegant wine rather than an explosive heavyweight. And speaking of natural elegance, what better wine than a Chambolle-Musigny?

This has to be one of my favourite Burgundy reds. It recalls many warm memories, including that never-to-be-forgotten occasion back in 1990 when I had the privilege of tasting a Chambolle 1978 at the Clos-Vougeot. The wine's refinement exceeded all my expectations. Chambolle-Musigny Pinot Noir has a quality of expression that is the very epitome of elegance. A 5-6 year old wine reveals classical notes of raspberries, cherries and cherry stones punctuated by touches of spice. The palate is rounded, the structure is a model of precision and the length can be truly magnificent. A Chambolle will suit a variety of dishes if they have the right finesse. The balance in this particular combination relies on the smoothness of the braised sauce, the somewhat gamey texture of the duck and the velvety delicacy of the dish as a whole. The harmony is almost beyond words: suffice to say that one of the best Chambolle Crus is simply called Les Amoureuses (the lovers).

Other wines to go with this dish
Morey Saint-Denis
Vosne-Romanée
Sancerre Rouge (lightly wooded)
Saint-Emilion
Pomerol
Châteauneuf-du-Pape Rouge

Other dishes to go with this wine
Warm salad of potted oxtails
Spit-roasted Bresse chicken, potatoes and
   pan-fried ceps
Grilled top rump of Charolais beef
Roasted pheasant with Chinese artichokes
Soumaintrain cheese (not too mature)
   with bacon bread

The sommelier's selection
Château de Chambolle-Musigny
Domaine A.-F. Gros
Domaine Noellat
Domaine Robert Siruge
Domaine Roumier

MADIRAN
potted duck with lentils

AOC
Madiran
REGION
**South West
France**
RED WINE
AREA
1,200ha
CULTIVARS
**Mainly:
Tannat
Also:
Cabernet-
Sauvignon
Cabernet-Franc
Fer Servadou**

Potted duck comes traditionally from the South West of France, but is now a popular favourite throughout the country, especially in winter. This dense, somewhat rustic-tasting dish does however need a wine that can stand up to it – anything too soft would pale by comparison.

There is something wonderfully smooth-tasting about a potted duck with lentils, despite the fibrous, compact texture of the meat. The best lentils for this dish if you can get them are firm, fine-skinned green Puy lentils that hold up well to prolonged cooking. This pungently traditional dish, unappealing as it is in summer, makes ideal winter fare washed down with a good strong red. Anything too discreet or over refined would be quite unsuitable. Your potted duck is a regional dish with a flourish – and it needs a wine of similar ilk. A Madiran, from the same region, fits the bill perfectly.

For many years, the Madiran's image suffered from a certain confusion of rusticity and strength. But these past 20 years have seen significant improvements in the wines of South West France, thanks to the efforts of local winegrowers. Today, that commitment to quality has paid off and the region now boasts a number of very respectable wines. The Tannat, which is the local cultivar, produces dark red, deep and powerful wines that can withstand prolonged aging. Its nose has a captivating complexity of smoky, spicy, almost animal notes of game and pepper. I am particularly fond of the Madiran as it begins to evolve – in which case, it needs to breathe in the decanter to soften its tannins (as you meanwhile admire its wonderfully dark colour). A Madiran – full-bodied, chewy, tannic and well structured – has all the build you need for potted duck and lentils. Indeed, the dish's somewhat rich, mouthfilling consistency actually sets off the denseness of the wine – creating an alliance of power and generosity that is almost spell-binding.

Other dishes to go with this wine
Sautéed foie gras deglazed with vinegar
Duck with lentils, duckling with cabbage
Cassoulet (white bean and meat stew)
Coq au vin
Pan-fried calf's liver with balsamic vinegar
Mixed brochettes (lamb, beef,
    kidneys, peppers)
Roast Pyrenean lamb with herbs
Young partridge, cabbage and prune stuffed
Hare à la Royale (with foie gras, truffles
    and/or quenelles, etc)
Jugged young wild boar
Jugged izard (Pyrenean wild goat)
Marinated venison
Pyrenean sheep's cheese and black cherry jam

Other wines to go with this dish
Irouléguy Rouge
Pécharmant
Bergerac
Cahors
Gigondas or St Joseph (both red)
Bandol Rouge
Vin de Corse Figari
Rioja (Spain)

The sommelier's selection
Chapelle Lenclos
Château Bouscassé
Château d'Aydie
Château Laffitte-Teston
Domaine Moureou

SAINT-EMILION
pigeon with cabbage

AOC
Saint-Emilion
REGION
Bordeaux
RED WINE
AREA
1,425ha
CULTIVARS
Mainly:
Merlot
Cabernet-
Sauvignon
Cabernet-Franc
Also:
Bouchet
Malbec

Cooking this dish isn't easy because on the one hand the pigeon must not be overdone, and on the other hand the cabbage needs prolonged stewing to remove its bitterness. The flavours hover between noble game and rustic vegetable, which makes the choice of wine more difficult than you might imagine.

This is a dish with power. There is the pungent taste of the sometimes acrid vegetable, left to steep for hours in the pigeon flavours. And there is the dense, almost gamey flesh of the noble bird itself (with the cabbage, I like it medium-rare). But providing you cook it correctly – removing the pigeon when it's done and leaving the cabbage to stew – what you get is an extremely tasty, almost roguish dish, with a combination of delicate textures and animal-like flavours.

A dish like this needs a succulent, caressing wine but one that retains plenty of fruit character. An overly fluid red doesn't stand a chance, while a very tannic wine might seem even harder alongside the acidic cabbage. A fairly spirited wine on the other hand might well strike the right balance. This doesn't necessarily mean heading for a sun-drenched terroir: Saint-Emilion will do nicely. I can think of no better match for our pigeon than a wine from the albeit diverse Saint-Emilion appellation. Whatever their different styles, Saint-Emilion wines all tend to be dense, rounded and velvety with plump tannins that go beautifully with this dish. The Merlot-based Saint-Emilion is always powerful but never too much so, taking full advantage of the Atlantic freshness of its terroir and the velvety texture of its main cultivar. The wine's cushiony elegance seems to envelope the ripe, stewed consistency of the cabbage and the fine, compact texture of the meat. The harmony in the fruity aromas of the wine is echoed in the flavours of the cabbage steeped in pigeon juices (but be sure to choose a youngish Saint-Emilion, around 5-7 years old).

The sommelier's selection
Château Angelus
Château Canon
Château Canon La Gaffelière
Château Chauvin
Château Cheval Blanc
Château Faugères
Château Figeac
Château Larmande
Château Moulin Saint-Georges
Château Pavie
Château Troplong Mondot
Château La Couspaude

Other wines to go with this dish
Saint-Joseph Rouge
Marsannay Rouge
Fixin
Gevrey-Chambertin
Toscani Merlot (Italy)

Other dishes to go with this wine
Roast duck with olive butter
Coq au vin
Roasted capon Bordeaux-style
Beef fillet in a crust with mushrooms
Marinated lamb with herbs
Leg of lamb with flageolets
Saint-Nectaire, Mimolette Etuvée, Reblochon

MARGAUX
roast goose sarlat-style

AOC
Margaux
REGION
Bordeaux
RED WINE
AREA
1,350ha
CULTIVARS
Mainly:
Merlot
Cabernet-
Sauvignon
Cabernet-Franc
Also:
Carmenère
Malbec
Petit-Verdot

This festive dish plays on the contrast between the crispy skin and rather fatty meat of the goose, served with a potato and mushroom accompaniment that will cushion the tannins of a fine but powerfully structured wine.

Roast goose, if regularly basted throughout cooking, has a wonderfully succulent texture. But rarely is it quite as melt-in-the-mouth as in this recipe from Sarlat in the South West of France. The addition of the potatoes, ceps and truffles sautéed in the goose fat works wonders with this bird. Such a generous dish might seem to invite a powerful wine but I would go for a more subtle combination. It takes a wine of refinement and elegance to bring out the succulent blend of texture and aroma in this dish.

You have a number of options here, especially if you choose a Médoc wine, but for me only the Margaux comes close to ideal. These elegant, airy, unbelievably subtle wines combine the suppleness of the Merlot with the robust structure typical of Cabernet-based reds. The exceptionally silky tannins and long, lingering palate of a Margaux have a natural affinity for juicy, even fleshy dishes. What you should not serve with a Margaux are green vegetables, because they make the wine seem watery, or very spicy sauces that spoil its delicacy. For roast goose with ceps and truffles, a mature Margaux is my first choice. The forest-floor aromas of the wine harmonise immediately with the irresistible scent of the truffles, and the tannins in this almost velvety wine naturally soak up the richness of the juice. Bear in mind however that variety is one of the greatest strengths of the exceptional Margaux appellation. Be sure to choose the right cru to go with the dish.

Other wines to go with this dish
Red wines:
Saint-Estèphe
Haut-Médoc
Canon-Fronsac (aged at least 10 years)
Pécharmant
Volnay
White wines (aged 10 years):
Pessac-Léognan
Puligny-Montrachet
Meursault
Hermitage

Other dishes to go with this wine
Lampreys Bordeaux-style
Quail roasted in its own juices
Roast guinea fowl or young partridge
with soft spices
Crispy poultry wings with soft spices
Rib of beef with bone marrow
Cheeses: Brillat-Savarin, Pierre-Robert,
Saint-Nectaire Fermier

The sommelier's selection
Château Labégorce Zédé
Château Margaux
Château Rauzan-Segla
Château Monbrison
Château Palmer
Château Siran

POMMARD
grilled rib of beef with pepper sauce and pommes paillasson

AOC
Pommard
REGION
Burgundy
RED WINE
AREA
210ha
CULTIVAR
Pinot Noir

There is an almost roguish quality about this explosively flavourful dish of parsley-flavoured beef, steeped in smoky grilled aromas and seasoned with pepper sauce. The wine you choose must stand up to this intensity of aroma.

I like rib of beef with a slightly piquant pepper sauce, plus a few drops of Balsamic vinegar to add a sweet and sour quality. And what better accompaniment to enhance the variety of textures in this dish than pommes paillasson: thin patties of grated raw potatoes sautéed in a small frying pan until crisp on the outside and soft on the inside. Rib of beef prepared in this way is so rich in flavour that finding a suitable wine shouldn't be too difficult.

A Pommard is a Cru Noble from the Côte de Beaune that combines superbly with grilled rib of beef. Wine and dish are magnificently complementary. The rich, tight texture of the meat mirrors the powerful structure of the wine, while the peppery flavours of the sauce are echoed by the spicy aromas of the Pommard, marked by touches of black fruits, pepper and smoke. These dense, sometimes slightly rustic but never inelegant wines express as many different nuances as there are crus and slopes in this famously diverse appellation. I am always struck by the many fine distinctions in Pommard wines. But what I particularly like about them is their spirit: that distinctive combination of aromatic expression, long palate and good aging potential. When serving a Pommard with grilled rib of beef, I think the power of the wine is more manageable if drunk on the cold side (17°C/62.6°F), after a short decanting (not more than an hour).

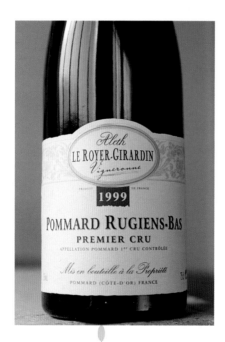

Other wines to go with this dish
Nuits-Saint-Georges Rouge
Gevrey-Chambertin
Cornas
Bandol Rouge
Coteaux du Languedoc Rouge
Faugères Rouge
Saint-Chinian Rouge
Toro (Spain)
Valpolicella Classico (Italy)

Other dishes to go with this wine
Corsican coppa on sesame toast
Mountain charcuterie (smoked)
Lamb with spices
Pork cheek stew with pepper sauce
Venison Grand Veneur
Large mushrooms stuffed with minced ham
Cheeses: Burgundian Soumaintrain, Citeaux,
Amour-de-Nuits; Livarot, Pont-L'Evêque
  (soft cheeses)

The sommelier's selection
Domaine Jean-Marc Boillot
Domaine de Courcel
Domaine Parent
Domaine Rebourgeon-Mure
Domaine Le Royer Girardin

CAHORS

beef wellington with mushrooms, artichokes and blackcurrant juice

AOC
Cahors
REGION
South West France
RED WINE
AREA
4,250ha
CULTIVARS
Mainly: Auxerrois (the local name for Malbec and Côt) Also: Tannat Merlot

The choice of wine here is determined by the sheer variety of ingredients in the dish: a succulent fillet of beef wrapped in flaky pastry, served with a garnish of artichokes bases, lightly seasoned with garlic then moistened with the cooking juices that are flavoured with blackcurrant juice.

This dish may seem a little confusing at first with its notes of baking from the golden flaky crust, the sweetness of the quartered artichokes bases and that hint of blackcurrant sharpness. The array of aromas continues inside the crust where sliced mushrooms (or truffles, why not?) add their own inimitable fragrance. The wine you choose has to harmonize on several levels: structure, substance and aroma. You are looking for a red wine with fruity, floral notes that have evolved towards deliciously welcome scents of the forest floor. It can't be too fluid, or it would clash with the flaky pastry, but it has to be silky enough to complement the texture of the meat. The distinctly vegetal taste of the artichokes can be a problem too, tending to make a wine seem rather metallic. Thankfully, we have the blackcurrant sauce to unite the flavours.

A Cahors from South West France will work beautifully in this combination. These wines, though once thought carelessly made, have improved significantly in recent years. They are usually dense and well coloured, with a black-fruit nose of violets and liquorice that echoes the aromas in the dish. In terms of structure, a Cahors has enough dense, even fleshy substance to hold its own against the tight texture of the roast beef. Cahors wines are often served with truffles (also from the South West) in which case you are best off with a 5-7 year old wine that retains its youthful fruitiness but also has that hint of humus that comes with age. It will combine effortlessly with this dish, if decanted an hour beforehand and served at 18°C (64.4°F).

Other wines to go with this dish
Gaillac Rouge
Pécharmant
Saint-Emilion
Côtes de Castillon
Bordeaux Côtes de Francs Rouge
Barolo, Barberesco, Gattinara
(Piedmont, Italy)

Other dishes to go with this wine
Platter of charcuterie
Potted giblets salad, blackcurrant sauce
Pigeon, pheasant or partridge in cocotte
    with wild mushrooms
Roast top rump of beef
Grilled beef entrecôte
Cassoulet Toulouse-style
Cheeses: Brebis des Pyrénées with
    blackcurrants, Rocamadour
Red berry batter pudding
Blackcurrant crumble

The sommelier's selection
Château du Cèdre
Château Goutoul
Château La Caminade
Château Lagrezette
Clos Triguedina

BANDOL ROUGE

daube de bœuf (beef stew) provençale-style with black olives

AOC
Bandol
REGION
Provence
RED WINE
This AOC also
produces
60% rosés and
5% whites
AREA
Total 1,300ha
for the AOC
as a whole
CULTIVARS
Mainly:
Mourvèdre
Also:
Grenache
Cinsault
Syrah
Carignan

In this traditional family dish from Provence, the beef is stewed with vegetables and herbs, plus regional black olives to add richness. The olives also provide the perfect link with the wine.

For me, Daube Provençale signifies evening meals with family or friends. This long-cooked, typically regional dish plays on the varied textures of the meat pieces –lean and fat, firm and tender – and the different tastes of the vegetables. The sauce is the unifying factor with its smooth but solid consistency and distinctive smack of black olives. A Bandol Rouge is the logical choice for this dish. First, because what you need here is a terroir combination and Bandol is one of the oldest-established Provencal vineyards. Second, because the complex aromas of a Bandol include notes of black-fruits, musk, spices and most particularly olives, chiming beautifully with the slightly bitter hint of olives in the dish.

I love Bandol Rouge for its rounded, generous, energetic character, good backbone and chewy mouthfeel. It has tannins that remain firm after 18 months cask aging, plus all the power, length and density of the Mourvèdre (its principal cultivar). Given these characteristics, a Bandol is best decanted an hour and a half before serving. It also takes a while to reach its prime, but around five years aging will see it good and ready to take on a Daube Provencale. The best vintage Bandols can age for considerably more than that, much longer in fact than most people think. I was once at a birthday dinner where the Bandol we were drinking with our daube had just turned 30, like one of the birthday guests. The year was a deliberate choice – and it proved to me that these wines can make it to 30 or more with no difficulty.

Other dishes to go with this wine
With a 2-4 year old wine:
Grilled red mullet
Bonito steak coated with blue poppy
   seeds in red wine sauce
Stuffed baby vegetables Nice-style
Ham and mushroom pizza
Lasagne Bolognaise
   With a 5-7 year old wine:
Duckling with olives
Glazed duckling with Cantonese rice
Osso bucco with tomato sauce
Spicy caramelised spare ribs
   With a very old wine:
Coffee-flavoured crème brûlée

Other wines to go with this dish
Les Baux de Provence Rouge
Gigondas Rouge
Châteauneuf-du-Pape Rouge
Californian reds based on the Syrah
   and/or the Grenache
South Australian wines based on the
   Syrah and the Cabernet-Sauvignon

The sommelier's selection
Château de Pibarnon
Château Pradeaux
Château Vannières
Domaine de Terrebrune
Domaine Lafran-Veyroles
Domaine Tempiers

WHITE BEER

veal escalope with citrus fruits and chicory

The choice you have when it comes to beer allows some highly inventive food combinations. This one is no exception – white beer and a veal escalope with citrus fruits and braised chicory.

The citrus element in this dish – preferably clementines – is essential to temper the almost ligneous firmness of the veal escalope and the bitterness of the virtually dry-braised chicory. The meat, sauce and vegetables provide varied structure together with a highly original combination of aromas in which the sauce plays a key role. The sauce is made by deglazing the pan with beer then adding a touch of cream. This serves to soften the contrasts and provide a gentle link between the different ingredients. Now for the choice of beer. Personally, I have always been more of a wine man myself but I was determined to get to know beer and especially beer cuisine. With help from the breweries, I tried out all sorts of beer and food combinations and made a number of interesting discoveries. Beer for instance does go very well with chocolate (even for someone like me who doesn't really like beer on its own). Brown ale goes well with a spicy, plain chocolate dessert. White beer goes with milk chocolate and praline. Whisky-flavoured beer (made with peated 'whisky malt') goes with black, whisky-flavoured chocolate. Another combination worth trying is amber beer with cumin and honey flavoured Munster cheese. For sheer consistency of taste, the most logical choice with veal escalope and citrus fruits is a young, white, unfiltered and naturally made beer, served at around 7-8°C (44.6-45.4°F). Its mousse-like consistency will echo the creaminess of the sauce while its refreshing but not overly bitter taste will marry well with the citrus notes in the sauce and the hint of bitterness in the chicory. Food and beer here complement each other perfectly, in a tranquil combination that avoids any violent contrast.

Other dishes to go with white beer
Rabbit terrine in aspic with grelot onions
Pan-fried scallops with citrus sauce
Sautéed pork marinated in beer with
   broad beans
Braised chicory and leeks
Cheeses: ash-coated goat's cheese
   (Sainte-Maure, Pyramide de Valençay);
   Brousse aux Herbes
Caramelised zabaglione with exotic fruits
   in beer
Peppery pineapple carpaccio with vanilla
   ice-cream

Wines to go with this dish
Chassagne-Montrachet Blanc
Chablis Premier Cru
Montlouis Sec
Vin de Corse Blanc
Marlborough Chardonnay
   (New Zealand)

The sommelier's selection
Blanche de Météor, Brasserie Météor
Colomba, Brasserie Pietra
Amadéus Blanche d'Abbaye, Brasseurs de Gayant
Blanche de Namur, Brasserie de Saint-Omer
Whitebread, Brasserie Interbrew France
Blanche de Cambrai, Brasserie La Choulette
Wieckse Witte, Brasserie Heineken

ALSACE RIESLING VENDANGES TARDIVES
blanquette de veau (veal stew) old-fashioned style

AOC
Alsace Riesling
REGION
Alsace
WHITE
MOELLEUX WINE
**This AOC also
produces dry
white wines**
AREA
**Total 3,350ha
for the AOC
as a whole**
CULTIVAR
Riesling

Blanquette de veau à l'ancienne was a great classic in our grandparents' time. The success of this dish lies in the melt-in-the-mouth texture of the long-cooked meat and the smoothness of the white sauce. Were it not for the egg (which is used as binding) this would be an easy dish to combine with wine.

Blanquette de veau à l'ancienne takes me back to my childhood. It was one my grandmother's favourite recipes and one of the first dishes I ever tried to combine with a wine. This is a stew that plays on velvetiness. The somewhat gelatinous texture of the meat (cubed shoulder, flank and brisket) merges with the melt-in-the-mouth garnish of baby vegetables and the creamy sauce made with cream and egg yoke plus a dash of lemon to add sharpness. The smoothness of the dish needs a softly sweet wine, although not so sweet as to be cloying. A red wine is out of the question because it would taste metallic alongside the egg.

An Alsace Riesling Vendanges Tardives was, once again, one of my grandmother's suggestions. From the moment I tasted it with her creamy blanquette I could see that this was an ideal combination. The Riesling has just the right body, substance and sweetness to match the texture of the dish. At the same time, its powerful mineral edge makes for a complex range of aromas together with a good crisp finish that is just what you need with a blanquette. Ideally the wine should be sweet (moelleux) but not syrupy (liquoreux). So we are probably talking about a Riesling that has aged for at least five years and lost some of its sweetness in the process ('mangé son sucre', as French winegrowers say). Served cool but not cold (12°C /53.6°F) it will marry beautifully with the blanquette, underscoring the flavours with a rich mineral crispness.

Other dishes to go with this wine
Pan-fried foie gras with onion purée
Cauliflower soufflé
Roast lobster or spiny lobster
Curried Dublin Bay prawns
Sliced, pan-fried porbeagle with a creamy,
   spice sauce
Bresse hen with cream
Cheeses: Munster, Livarot, Pont-L'Evêque,
   Tomme de Savoie-Abondance
Warm apple tart
Pear tarte Tatin (caramelised upside-down
   pear tart)
Poached pears with vanilla and sultanas
Chiboust cream with apricot halves

Other wines to go with this dish
Meursault
Chassagne-Montrachet Blanc
Savigny-Lès-Beaune Blanc
Monthélie Blanc
Savennières
Vouvray
Montlouis
Hermitage Blanc
Carneros Chardonnay (California, USA)
Barossa Valley Riesling (South Australia)

The sommelier's selection
Domaine du Weinbach-Faller
Domaine Zind Humbrecht
Maison Trimbach

COTE-ROTIE

pan-fried calf's liver with raspberry vinegar and blackcurrants

AOC
Côte-Rôtie
REGION
Rhône Valley
RED WINE
AREA
200ha
CULTIVARS
Mainly:
Syrah
Also:
Viognier

With that slightly bitter-taste of pan-fried calf's liver and the measured acidity of the vinegar and blackcurrants, this intensely fragrant dish presents quite a challenge when it comes to the choice of wine.

As every lover of calf's liver knows – overcooking toughens the delicate texture of calf meat, destroying its characteristically melt-in-the-mouth, almost mousse-like consistency. Another distinguishing if less attractive feature of calf's liver is a tendency to bitterness. You overcome that problem by deglazing the pan with raspberry vinegar (that loses its acidity in the process). The blackcurrants are not so much a garnish as a much-needed touch of fruit, lending an acidulous sweetness that balances the flavours overall. The wine you need for such a dense yet refined dish is a silky, velvety red whose texture will bring out the smoothness of the liver. It must be strong but not too heady so as to marry well with the fruit fragrances.

A Côte-Rôtie offers just that combination of power and freshness. Côte-Rôtie wines are made from two cultivars, one red (the Syrah) and one white (the Viognier). They express the subtleties of their different terroirs with conspicuous elegance. It was Etienne Guigal – grandfather of Maison Guigal's current owner – who first introduced me to the secrets of this unique appellation. A young Côte-Rôtie has a black- and red-fruit nose combined with a spicy hint of pepper and a touch of smokiness from the time spent on wood. As it ages, it develops more complex aromas of truffles and the forest floor while retaining that airy, refreshing quality owed to the Viognier. This is a wine with exceptional aging potential. I recently had the privilege of tasting a 1947 Côte-Rôtie that was a marvel of aromatic maturity and sensual velvetiness. To my mind, a 10-year-old Côte-Rôtie is the ideal match for calf's liver. It should be decanted an hour and a half beforehand so as to bring out its black fruit bouquet and enhance the spicy notes typical of this appellation. Fruity notes and silky texture will then be a feature of wine and dish alike, making a combination that comes close to perfection.

Other dishes to go with this wine
Shavings of Parma ham
Pheasant terrine with truffle shavings
Pan-fried thrushes with gizzards
Grilled rib of beef with wild
   mushroom sauce
Veal fillet mignon with chanterelle
   mushrooms
Rack of lamb with herbs
Venison fillet (doe or buck) with fruit sauce
Cheeses: mature Saint-Marcellin,
   Picodon Sec with black olive bread
Crème brûlée flavoured with allspice
   and morellos

Other wines to go with this dish
Gigondas
Minervois-la-Livinière
Volnay
Santenay
Morey-Saint-Denis

The sommelier's selection
Château D'Ampuis Guigal
Domaine Burgaud
Domaine Clusel Roch
Domaine Duclaux
Domaine Jean-Michel Gerin
Domaine Jamet
Domaine Stephan

CHABLIS

andouillette with thick-cut chips

AOC
Chablis
REGION
Burgundy
WHITE WINE
AREA
2,780ha
CULTIVAR
Chardonnay

This elaborate, pungent sausage is practically an institution in the Chablis area of France. Serving it in a Chablis-based sauce will soften its peppery, herby tang and create the perfect terroir combination.

There is no mistaking the aroma of an andouillette – this is a sausage that makes a pungently fragrant entry. The texture on the palate can take you back a bit too, with that more or less succulent mixture of lean and fatty minced meat, liberally flavoured with herbs. You can of course barbecue andouillettes but I find this brings out their smoky taste, making them more difficult to combine with a fine wine. With a Chablis, I like to pan-fry them and serve with a garnish of crispy, thick-cut chips to help soak up the sauce. Use a Chardonnay-based white wine for the sauce, preferably a nice little Chablis with a good smattering of acidulous notes to offset the richness of the sausage.

I was with that seminal Chablis producer François Raveneau when I first tasted this combination. Until then, I had always reserved Chablis for seafood, with which it combines perfectly thanks to its natural affinity for iodised flavours. A Chablis expresses the qualities of a very particular terroir, possessing good mineral backbone and that famous taste of gunflint that goes so well with the taste of the sea. It is also a very complex wine with its notes of orchard fruits and flowers (honeysuckle and particularly hawthorn, sometimes with a hint of verbena), even if it can seem a bit thin at times on account of that biting mineral edge. You need a fairly intense Chablis for andouillettes (a Fourchaume or Vaillons Premier Cru, for instance), one past the first flush of youth (3-4 years' aging will do), served at around 10°C (50°F). Decant it by all means – and take the opportunity to admire the greenish gold reflections of a wine that will fill out as it airs to become the perfect partner for andouillette.

Other wines to go with this dish
  White wines:
Mâcon
Saint-Joseph
Vouvray Sec
Wachau Grüner Veltliner (Austria)
Rheingau Riesling (Germany)
  Rosé and clairet wines:
Bordeaux Clairet
Fronton Rosé
Corbières Rosé
Tavel
Bandol Rosé
  Red wines:
Beaujolais
Gamay de Touraine
Sancerre
Arbois
Vin de Savoie Gamay

Other dishes to go with this wine
  With a 2-3 year old wine:
Flat oysters
Cockles in lemony aromatic broth
Frogs legs with parsley
Pan-fried scallops with sea salt
  With a five year + wine:
Roast king prawns
Thin fillets of sole with lemon butter
Roast hen with turnips
Osso bucco cooked in Chablis
Braised ham on the bone in Chablis sauce
Pan-fried chanterelle mushrooms
Dry goat's cheeses

The sommelier's selection
Cave La Chablisienne
Domaine Dauvissat
Domaine d'Élise
Domaine Raveneau
Domaine Jean-Paul Droin
Domaine Laroche
Domaine William Fèvre

PULIGNY-MONTRACHET BLANC
ham with epoisses cheese sauce

AOC
Puligny-Montrachet
REGION
Burgundy
WHITE WINE
This AOC also produces 2% reds
AREA
257ha given to whites (total 262ha)
CULTIVAR
Chardonnay

A sauce made with Epoisses cheese is, as you might imagine, often a bit strong for most wines. The ham in this dish should be served piping hot but the sauce should be barely warm, so as to restrain its fragrance and prevent it from spoiling the rest of the meal.

Hot roast ham is a classically regional dish from Burgundy where in some inns they still roast the meat in the traditional manner over a huge open hearth. This particular recipe owes its originality to the distinctive flavour of the Epoisses cheese used for the sauce. Epoisses is a strong-smelling Burgundy cheese that, once stripped of its washed rind, gives the sauce a remarkable texture. This dish always reminds me of weekends spent with fellow sommeliers just before the Hospices de Beaune auction in November. It conjures up visions of the autumn, of wine festivals and evenings with friends. Lightly garnished with sautéed potatoes or polenta cakes, a terroir dish like this invites a marriage of contrasts – something surprising but seductive. Roast ham is naturally suited to a white wine and for maximum impact I suggest we pair this simple rustic dish with that paragon of refinement, a Puligny-Montrachet. The Puligny AOC and its neighbour Chassagne are the home of the Grand Cru de Montrachet, the finest white wine in the world. Other sublime appellations in this area include Bâtard-Montrachet, Bienvenues-Bâtard-Montrachet and Chevalier-Montrachet – to mention but a few. A Puligny-Montrachet is a noble, honest, refined white wine that performs well within 3-4 years but can also withstand several decades of aging. A young Puligny-Montrachet (3-4 years old) shows good density and a structure not unlike a red wine. Daring it may be, but this combination with the ham will reveal all the spirit of the young wine. Its tannins will stand up to the firm texture of the warm ham, while that touch of vanilla from time spent in the cask will echo the smoky flavours of the meat. Above all, its fruity aromas (citrus fruits, exotic fruits, orchard fruits) and elegant mineral edge can hold out against the pungent smell of the hot Epoisses. Served at around 9°C (48.2°F), a Puligny complements rather than competes with the cheese, its mineral freshness and remarkable concentration adding an overall sense of refinement.

Other dishes to go with this wine
      With a 3-5 year old wine:
Shrimp tempura
Dublin Bay prawns with citrus fruits
Scallops with cream
Pike quenelles with white butter
Turbot or John Dory, Hollandaise sauce
      With a 5-10 year old wine (or older):
Lobster with saffron
Curried Dublin Bay prawns
Roast Bresse chicken
Veal escalopes with cream
White or black truffle risotto
Pan-fried chanterelle mushrooms
All goat's cheeses, Vacherin
Vanilla millefeuille

Other wines to go with this dish
      White wines:
Meursault
Beaujolais
Côtes du Jura
Côtes du Rhône
Alsace Pinot Gris
Chardonnay Toscano (Italy)
      Red wines:
Bourgogne Hautes-Côtes de Nuit
Bourgogne Hautes-Côtes de Beaune

The sommelier's selection
Domaine du Château de Puligny
Domaine Leflaive
Domaine Louis Carillon
Domaine Sauzet
Maison Louis Jadot

COTEAUX DU LANGUEDOC ROUGE
grilled spare ribs with roasted figs

AOC
Coteaux du
Languedoc
REGION
Languedoc
RED WINE
This AOC also
produces
12% whites and
13% rosés
AREA
7,500ha given to reds
(total 10,000ha)
CULTIVARS
Mainly:
Grenache
Mourvèdre
Syrah
Also:
Cinsault
Carignan

This simple but unmistakably roguish dish tastes even richer when liberally flavoured with herbs such as sage, thyme, bay leaf and rosemary. This is how they like to eat it in the Midi-Pyrénées where our grilled ribs and roasted figs take on a garrigue-like fragrance that we can also look for in a wine.

Barbecued pork spare ribs are a real gem of a summer recipe and a particular favourite of mine when eating al fresco with friends. There is however only one way to get all that deliciously smoky meat off the bone and that is to use your fingers. Ideally, the meat should be marinated for several hours beforehand in olive oil and herbs. The wine to go with it should be generous, fairly warm and unashamedly alcoholic. The meat if properly barbecued (rather than burnt) should have a firm, almost potted texture that can stand up to a tannic, foursquare wine with a powerful but sunny disposition. A Coteaux du Languedoc is ideal in this case. Given the sheer size of the appellation, these wines do vary considerably in style. Most of them however display strong character and a balance typical of their cultivars: the roundness of the Grenache, the rigorous structure of the Mourvèdre and the spicy fruit of the Syrah. The Coteaux du Languedoc from the Montpellier area (Pic Saint-Loup and the Saint-Drézéry vineyards) are particularly well suited to Mediterranean dishes, especially those that make a feature of herbs. Here we have a perfect match, the fragrance of the fresh roasted figs highlighting the garriguey aromas and fruity notes in the wine – a marriage of truly devastating allure that reaches beyond simple harmony.

Other dishes to go with this wine
With a 2-3 year old wine:
Poultry or game terrine
Brawn
Tuna tartar
Peppers stuffed with lamb
Pélardon des Cévennes (goat's cheese)
   with olive and herb bread; Niolo
   (soft Corsican cheese)
Cherry batter pudding
Flamed cherry jubilee with vanilla ice-cream
Blackberry, fig or prune tart
Plain chocolate fondant
Coffee millefeuille
   With a 5-6 year old wine:
Roast woodcock, young partridge or pigeon
Pigeon pastilla with figs
Thick beefsteak with bone marrow sauce
   or French brown sauce
Rib of beef with grilled vegetables
   (courgettes, pepper, onions)
Lamb chops with herbs
Lamb tagine with crystallised lemons

Other wines to go with this dish
Côtes de Provence Rouge
Côtes du Roussillon Rouge
Côtes du Roussillon-Villages Rouge
Penedes Tinto (Spain)
Chianti Classico (Italy)
Tancredi di Sicilia (Italy)

The sommelier's selection
Château de Capitoul
Château de l'Engarran
Clos Marie
Domaine d'Aupilhac
Domaine Durand Camillo
Domaine l'Hortus
Mas Bruguière
Mas Jullien

PAUILLAC

seven-hour leg of lamb with broad beans

AOC
Pauillac
REGION
Bordeaux
RED WINE
AREA
1,200ha
CULTIVARS
Mainly:
Merlot
Cabernet-
Sauvignon
Cabernet-Franc
Also:
Carmenère
Malbec
Petit Verdot

This ancient dish from Bordeaux requires some patience. The lamb is slow-cooked at a low temperature, acquiring a melt-in-the-mouth texture to which only a great red wine can do justice.

Seven-hour leg of lamb is so friable by the time you take it out of the oven that the meat can easily fall off the bone. So handle it with care as you place it on the garnish of fresh broad beans. The taste is a real treat but the lamb, reduced to an almost potted meat consistency, must be carefully chewed in order to release all of its flavours. A similarly chewy wine is de rigueur here. It must be powerful and refined, with elegant but very dense tannins, and a build capable of handling those vegetal, somewhat starchy notes in the beans as well as the full-bodied flavour of the dish as a whole.

The most satisfactory match I ever came across was in Bordeaux some years ago now when I met Baron Philippe de Rothschild for the first time. It was he who introduced me to the combination of a Vin de Pauillac with that other regional marvel of Médoc gastronomy, Pauillac lamb. Here was a traditional partnership of two terroir products that did things in style. The truth is that a Pauillac doesn't call for complicated dishes – it can almost stand on its own. In fact, it seems so powerful for the first 7-8 years that there isn't really any dish it goes with well. Increasing age makes it more amenable but nonetheless characterful. A mature Pauillac is sumptuously rounded, with notes of black and red fruits, spicy scents, touches of chocolate and liquorice and exceptional length on the palate. It is elegant and spirited, and has the substance, volume and presence on the palate to partner the heartiest fare.

Other wines to go with this dish
Saint-Estèphe
Premières Côtes de Blaye Rouge
Cahors
Châteauneuf-du-Pape Rouge
Côtes du Roussillon-Villages
Napa Valley Cabernet-Sauvignon
    (California, USA)
Maule Valley Cabernet-Sauvignon (Chile)

Other dishes to go with this wine
Pheasant terrine with juniper
Rack of lamb with ceps
Beef fillet in a crust with
    mushroom duxelles
Haunch of venison with chestnuts
Abbaye de Belloc (Pyrenean
    sheep's cheese)

The sommelier's selection
Château La Bécasse
Château La Tour
Château Lafite Rothschild
Château Lynch Bages
Château Pontet-Canet
Château Mouton Rothschild
Château Pichon Longueville
Château Pichon Longueville-Comtesse de Lalande

CHATEAUNEUF-DU-PAPE ROUGE

tapenade-stuffed saddle of lamb with roasted cherry tomatoes

AOC
Châteauneuf-du-
Pape
REGION
Rhône Valley
RED WINE
This AOC also
produces
5% whites
AREA
3,000ha given to
reds (total
3,200ha)
CULTIVARS
Mainly:
Grenache
Syrah
Mourvèdre
Cinsault
Also:
Terret
Muscardin
Vaccarèse
Counoise
Picardan

Lamb steeped in the pungent aromas of a black olive tapenade stuffing, combined with the acidulous sweetness of roasted tomatoes – for a wine lover like me, such contrasting flavours are a particularly challenging combination.

The dish itself is a subtle marriage of opposites, setting the bitterness of the olives against the acidity of the tomatoes, both thankfully tempered by cooking. The dish is best made with saddle of lamb, stuffed with tapenade so as to infuse it with the rich olive aromas, and roasted in a hot oven. The cherry tomatoes are roasted in the meat juices just long enough to concentrate their sweetness. As to the wine, it needs to match up to the dense, tight texture of the lamb. We want a balanced combination based on the complementary densities of the wine and meat – anything too fluid or understated would be a mistake.

A Châteauneuf-du-Pape has just the personality and spirit we need for this dish – far too much in fact for any very light or delicate dishes. This wine comes from a terroir renowned for its galets roulés (rolled pebbles) where the Grenache grape is in its element. The wines of Châteauneuf express all the density of the Grenache, together with notes of kirsch and chocolate and aromas of leather. Many of them also have a hint of black olives recalling the tapenade flavours in the lamb. This is a match that derives its build from the texture of the meat and the structure of the wine. Speaking as a fan of Châteauneuf-du-Pape wines, I recommend you decant them around an hour beforehand and serve at around 17°C (62.6°F). This will bring out their freshness with no loss of the silky velvetiness that is so typical of this appellation.

Other wines to go with this dish
Hermitage Rouge
Pommard
Chinon Rouge
Bourgueil Rouge
Anjou-Villages Rouge
Ribera del Duero from the Valladolid
    region (Spain)
New World Cabernet-Sauvignon and
    Syrah blends (Australia, Chile, USA)

Other dishes to go with this wine
Pheasant terrine
Truffles en papillotes with foie gras
Roast woodcock or thrush, flambé
    with Marc de Châteauneuf
Jugged wild rabbit
Beef fillet with truffles
Venison fillet with chestnuts
Haunch of venison with olives
Wild mushroom fricassee

The sommelier's selection
Réserve des Célestins
Château de Beaucastel
Château de la Nerthe
Château de Lagardine
Château Rayas
Clos des Papes
Domaine du Vieux Télégraphe
Domaine de la Janasse

AJACCIO ROUGE
roast kid with chestnuts

AOC
Ajaccio
REGION
Corsica
RED WINE
This AOC also
produces
10% whites and
40% rosés
AREA
100ha given to
reds (total 205ha)
CULTIVARS
Mainly:
Sciacarello
Also:
Barbarossa
Niellucio
Grenache
Cinsault

Tender young kid, pit-roasted whole in the Méchoui style, is a favourite spring dish in Corsica. The meat is flavoured with herbs and basted regularly with the cooking juices, taking on a variety of flavours and textures that will taste even better with the right wine.

Roast kid with chestnuts has all the fragrance of the Corsican garrigue. On the palate, the crispy succulent meat contrasts deliciously with the soft, slightly starchy flesh of the chestnut garnish. This tasty dish does depend on good-quality ingredients but it isn't difficult to pair with a wine. A regional match is called for here – and what could be more perfectly suited to goat than an Ajaccio Rouge? Geography has something to do with it, but by no means everything. This is a wine with the power and generosity of the Mediterranean but there is also a subtle, discreet side to its character. Its light colour is evidence of its moderate concentration, a feature that limits its warmth without dulling its personality. An Ajaccio Rouge is born of a sun-drenched, limestone terroir, and offers a delightful combination of roundness and finesse. It is complex on the nose, with aromas of leather and the forest floor plus notes of kirsch and stoned fruits. Contrary to received opinion, it is also perfectly capable of aging. I recently tasted a 1959 Ajaccio Rouge that remained as fragrant as ever, with gorgeous aromas of the garrigue, and nuts and crystallised quince. When serving it with kid, the only special requirement is not to drink it too warm, say around 16°C (60.8°F). Keeping it on the cool side will conserve all of its fruit, and create a most successful match based on those qualities that wine and dish have in common: a mellow texture and that unmistakable fragrance of the garrigue.

Other wines to go with this dish
Arbois Rouge
Chianti Classico (Italy)
Vino Nobile di Montepulciano (Italy)

Other dishes to go with this wine
Coppa and other Corsican charcuterie
Roast leg of lamb with herbs
Jugged fillet of young wild boar
Beef stew Provençale
Sicilian Caponata
Dry Brocciu (Corsican cheese)

The sommelier's selection
Clos Capitoro
Clos d'Alzeto
Domaine Comte Peraldi

HERMITAGE ROUGE
jugged hind with mushrooms

AOC
Hermitage
REGION
Rhône Valley
RED WINE
**This AOC also
produces
20% whites**
AREA
**100ha given
to reds
(total 125ha)**
CULTIVAR
Syrah

Jugged hind (female deer) is a hearty, complex dish much sought-after in the autumn by lovers of game. It is cooked in a wine-based marinade flavoured with herbs and a strained sauce that is traditionally thickened with blood.

Making jugged hind requires patience and expertise. The long-marinated meat must be slow-cooked so as to infuse it with the steeping liquid, leaving the preparation of the sauce until last. In the autumn, wood mushrooms - pan-fried separately – are a natural complement to this much-prized and extremely tasty dish for special occasions. Speaking as a lover of game in all its forms, I like to drink a dense, powerful wine with jugged hind, one with just a hint of animal about it. An Hermitage Rouge is a perfect example. This magnificent wine from the Rhône Valley gives one of its finest performances when paired with game. With jugged hare, an Hermitage Rouge around 10 years old creates a match of splendidly complex harmony. The wine has all the elegance required by such an intensely tasty yet very refined dish: aromas of macerated fruit, truffles, humus and liquorice but also good length on the palate thanks to its handsome mineral core and refined tannins. A young Hermitage (10 years is young for these wines) retains noticeably fruity scents of violets and red berries. Its roasted, spicy notes meanwhile take on a slightly gamy edge that echoes to perfection the tender meat of the jugged hare. On the palate, meat and wine strike a well-judged balance of firmness and velvetiness, roundness and density, elegance and power. As it ages, an Hermitage Rouge naturally takes on a brownish-orange hue while its texture grows more supple. I prefer it then with plain roasted feathered game – garnish with a few truffles and you have a dish to die for.

Other dishes to go with this wine
With an 8-10 year old wine:
Raviolis de Royan with champignons
de Paris in cream
Foie gras and truffle turnover
Ducking with black olives
Peppered fillet of beef
Tournedos Rossini
Tournedos with black olives
Entrecôte in wine merchant sauce
Rack of lamb with herbs
Kidneys in port
Dauphiné-style potatoes au gratin
Chinese artichokes sautéed in butter
Mature Saint-Marcellin cheese, olive bread
With a 10 year + wine:
Roast pheasant or thrush, garnished
with truffles

Other wines to go with this dish
Côte-Rôtie
Crozes-Hermitage Rouge
Vosne-Romanée
Chambolle-Musigny
Volnay
Pomerol
Saint-Emilion
Barolo (Italy)
Oregon Pinot Noir (USA)

The sommelier's selection
Domaine Jean-Louis Chave
Domaine des Remizières
Maison Delas
Maison Chapoutier
Maison Paul Jaboulet Aîné

FITOU

jugged boar with chestnut purée

AOC
Fitou
REGION
Languedoc
RED WINE
AREA
2,500ha
CULTIVARS
Mainly:
Carignan
Also:
Grenache
Mourvèdre
Syrah

Robust, highly seasoned, powerfully gamy – jugged boar is traditional fare for a hunting weekend. Prepared 24 hours in advance, it retains a pungently high flavour that tastes all the better for the mildness of the chestnut purée.

For me, wild boar conjures up warm memories of autumn weekends spent with fellow game lovers. I love long-cooked meats like this with that stewed texture they get after simmering for hours in a thick, tasty sauce. In this particular dish, some of the meat pieces (from different parts of the boar) are more succulent than others but they all tend to taste fairly high. The sauce includes ingredients such as juniper berries that recall the animal's natural environment. If sufficiently smooth and fragrant, it will temper the animal pungency of the meat. Sometimes at these hunting dinners I will serve a wine that isn't a great classic. A venerable Burgundy would of course be ideal. But so too would a less obvious, more original wine that brings a touch of joyousness to the table. A Fitou for instance, makes a delightful accompaniment to our boar and has just the jovial, robust qualities we need for this match. It is warm and powerful, with aromas of macerated fruits that hint of game, plus notes of over-ripe black fruit and touches of spice. A Fitou from one of the inland vineyards (rather than along the coast) has a solid, foursquare build that is particularly well suited to the firm texture of the sauce-coated meat. I usually decant the wine shortly before serving (no more than 45 minutes beforehand to avoid the risk of oxidation). It then becomes the perfect accomplice for our boar, neither vying for power nor deadening the taste buds – a sunny combination that adds a fanciful touch to any hunting evening.

Other dishes to go with this wine
Poultry or game terrine
Salad of smoked duck breasts
Salad of potted gizzards
Grilled sardines
Duck with olives
Beef goulash
Stew with black olives
Pot-au-feu
Chile con carne with red kidney beans
Ripe Chabichou, black olive bread
Chocolate tart with griottines
Crisp praline dessert with sauce Arabica

Other wines to go with this dish
Corbières Rouge
Côtes du Roussillon-Villages
Priorat (Spain)
Toro (Spain)

The sommelier's selection
Château de Nouvelles
Domaine les Mille Vignes
Domaine Bertrand Berge
Producteurs du Mont Tauch

NUITS-SAINT-GEORGES ROUGE
venison grand veneur with celery chips

AOC
Nuits-Saint-Georges
REGION
Burgundy
RED WINE
This AOC also produces 2% whites
AREA
300ha given to reds (total 305ha)
CULTIVAR
Pinot Noir

Here we have a meeting of two giants of French gastronomy – venison cooked in an ultra-classical French style, combined with the magnificent Burgundy that gave its name to the famous Côtes de Nuits.

Venison has all the nobility of big game, rich in flavour with tender, firm, yet succulent flesh. The Grand Veneur sauce (essentially a sauce poivrade enriched with red wine) tempers the strong-flavoured meat, adding creaminess and velvetiness to the dish as a whole. A sprinkling of redcurrants just before serving introduces a peppery, acidulous note of fresh berries. The garnish need not be quite so classical. For this recipe, we add a touch of softness with an accompaniment of sliced celery chips.

With such a complex dish, it has to be a great red wine and what obviously springs to mind is a Nuits-Saint-Georges. There are a number of suitable choices of course but I am particularly fond of Nuits-Saint-Georges – perhaps because it was also my parents' favourite wine. Whatever the case, this is a wine with the density and smoothness of the Pinot Noir that takes on gamy notes as it ages.

But you can't hurry a Nuits-Saint-Georges. It needs at least five years' aging to express itself properly and should be decanted before serving. Better still, pour it straight from the bottle into large Burgundy glasses and leave it to open up at a temperature of 18°C (64.4°F). This will play down the aromas overall, leaving you free to enjoy an ultra-powerful but also very refined combination.

Other wines to go with this dish
Pommard
Vosne-Romanée
Châteauneuf-du-Pape Rouge
Côte-Rôtie
Pomerol
Saint-Emilion
Barbaresco (Italy)
Vino Nobile di Montepulciano (Italy)
Rioja (Spain)
Penedes (Spain)

Other dishes to go with this wine
Duck ham on toast with fresh redcurrants
Boar's head
Rib of beef with wine merchant sauce
Entrecôte with wild mushrooms
Cheeses: Laguiole, Morbier, Saint-Nectaire

The sommelier's selection
Clos de l'Arlot
Domaine Prieuré Roch
Maison Faiveley

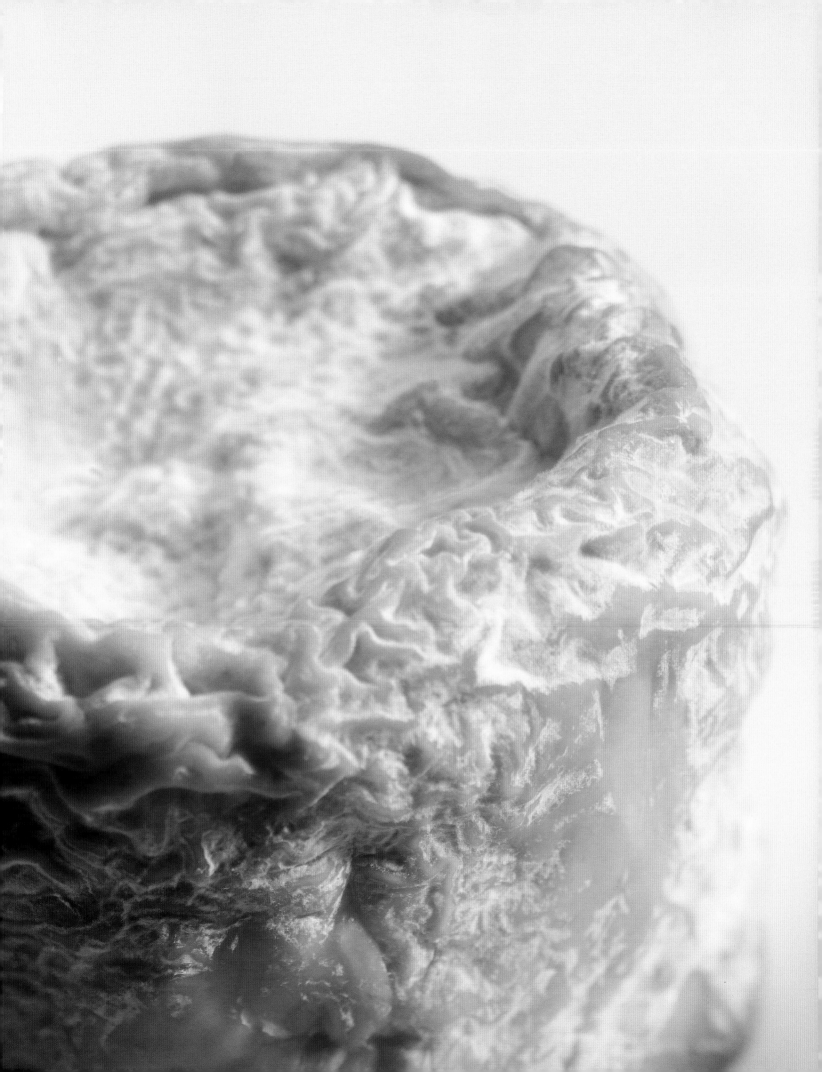

ALSACE TOKAY-PINOT GRIS
stuffed cabbage with mild spices

AOC
Alsace Tokay-Pinot Gris
REGION
Alsace
WHITE WINE
This AOC also produces moelleux and liquoreux wines
AREA
1,350ha
CULTIVAR
Pinot Gris

Green vegetables rarely go well with wine. Their pronounced vegetal flavour gives red wine a metallic taste while their watery consistency tends to make wine seem thin. Things are not quite so difficult with a dish like this, in which the cabbage is stuffed with rice and mild spices.

The first thing to point out with this recipe is that 'mild spices' does not mean chilli. The blanched cabbage leaves are simply filled with rice that is seasoned with paprika, allspice and other exotic spices, then rolled up and cooked in a cocotte. As it cooks, the cabbage loses its bitter-tasting, crunchy texture, becoming succulently soft and distinctly tasty.

Red wines, unless extremely tender, are to be avoided with a dish like this – a crisp, nicely fragrant white is much more suitable. To my mind, the ideal choice with stuffed cabbage rolls is an Alsace Tokay-Pinot Gris, a more original match than some of the better-known whites. This is a wine with a nose of preserved fruits and exotic spices, together with an elegant blend of aromatic intensity and soft, mineral notes that suits mild-flavoured foods. I am especially fond of the dry version of Alsace Tokay-Pinot Gris (which retains some residual sweetness). This food and wine combination relies as much on texture – succulent cabbage, creamy stuffing, smooth wine – as spicy aroma (another reason not to over-season the stuffing). Served at 9°C (48.2°F) the very particular varietal flavours of an Alsace Tokay-Pinot Gris are sure to flatter a dish of stuffed cabbage rolls.

Other dishes to go with this wine
Poppy seed or cheese vol-au-vents
   (aperitif)
Snails in puff pastry
Scallops in aromatic broth with leeks
Glazed poultry wings
Chicken and grapes in a beggar's purse
   (made with brick pastry)
Pigeon pastilla
Chicken Chinese-style with almonds
   and cashew nuts
Cheeses: Maroilles, Livarot, Pont-L'Evêque
Mendiant (dry chocolate cake topped with
   dried fruit) with vanilla crème brulée

Other wines to go with this dish
   White wines:
L'Etoile
Müller-Turghau Franken (Germany)
Red wines (tender):
Beaujolais Red
Côte Roannaise
Côteaux du Lyonnais

The sommelier's selection
Domaine Rolly Gassmann
Domaine Marc Tempé
Domaine Ernest Burn

PESSAC-LEOGNAN BLANC
curry-flavoured shrimp risotto

AOC
Pessac-Léognan
REGION
Bordeaux
WHITE WINE
**This AOC also
produces
80% reds**
AREA
**280ha given to
whites (total
1,350ha)**
CULTIVARS
**Mainly:
Sauvignon
Also:
Sémillon
Muscadelle**

A blissfully smooth Italian risotto provides a golden opportunity for a rounded, caressing wine. The wine's qualities are naturally enhanced by the texture of risotto – whether plain or flavoured as in this recipe.

The key to a good risotto is careful cooking, stirring those tiny grains continuously until they reach a soft, almost sticky consistency. In this recipe, the rice is cooked in fish stock then mixed with large peeled shrimps, curry spices and a touch of parmesan (to bring out the flavours). The overall taste should not be too spicy or it will detract from the elegance of the dish and, worse still, mask the taste of the wine.

I was in Japan when I first discovered the pleasures of a Pessac-Léognan Blanc with rice. This is dry Bordeaux wine at its finest: dense, fleshy and elegant with assertive mineral notes and classy wood. The texture displays an almost mellow quality, owed to the varietal character of the Sémillon, that goes particularly well with rice. The intense nose, with its distinctive Sauvignon freshness, serves to balance the pronounced curry flavours. The synergy on the palate comes close to perfection, especially with a Pessac-Léognan that contains a high proportion of Sémillon. But do be careful not to over-chill the wine or you will stun its aromas and flavours and create a disagreeable contrast with the piping hot risotto.

Other dishes to go with this wine
Marinated shrimps
Crab-stuffed sea urchins
Shrimp tempura Japanese-style
Curried spiny lobster
Lobster American-style
Ink-stuffed baby squid
Sautéed scallops
Turbot with morel mushrooms
Thin fillets of sole with fried parsley
Rabbit in mustard sauce

Other wines to go with this dish
Jurançon Sec
Chardonnay de Limoux
Piemonte Chardonnay (Italy)
Sauvignon and Sémillon blends from
the Victoria region (Australia)

The sommelier's selection
Château La Garde
Château de Fieuzal
Château Smith Haut Laffitte
Château Larrivet-Haut-Brion
Château Coutins-Lurton
Château Malartic-Lagravière
Domaine de Chevalier

BORDEAUX CLAIRET
seafood lasagne

AOC
Bordeaux Clairet
REGION
Bordeaux
CLAIRET WINE
AREA
421ha
CULTIVARS
Mainly:
Merlot
Cabernet Franc
Cabernet-
Sauvignon
Also:
Carmenère
Malbec
Petit Verdot

Pasta with seafood plays a large part in Mediterranean cuisine, my own favourite being fresh lasagne steeped in the flavours of the filling. Flat pasta, in particular, has a divinely caressing texture on the palate.

There must be thousands of recipes for lasagne with seafood. Personally I like this one: lasagne cooked with clams, shrimps, mussels and scallops, seasoned with garlic and parsley, sprinkled with breadcrumbs, and browned in the oven. The sauce is made with dry white wine and cream - some people also add tomato. It starts off quite thin but thickens as the lasagne absorbs the liquid. The finished dish is a delectable combination of firm seafood and soft pasta, bathed in fragrant aromas with a whiff of the sea.

Bearing in mind these characteristics, there is only one wine that fits the bill and that is a Bordeaux Clairet. A red wine is unsuitable, while a white wine might well prove too fluid alongside this dish. A Bordeaux Clairet on the other hand, even more than a rosé, has a light tannic structure that will balance the smoothness of the pasta. Its airy, fruity, almost crisp freshness will meanwhile never be overcome by the lasagne. I am very fond of Bordeaux Clairet. For me, this is a wine typical of its origins: classical Bordeaux red cultivars and the maritime freshness of the Atlantic. Don't be put off if at first the wine seems rather too fluid with your lasagne: its precise tannins support a decently long finish. This original but under-rated wine does in fact perform well with all sorts of dishes and in all sorts of circumstances. As to age and temperature, choose a young wine (2-3 years old) and serve at around 12°C (53.6°F).

Other wines to go with this dish
   Rosé wines:
Tavel
Fronton
Béarn
Chinon
Cerasuolo di Abruzzo (Italy)
Chiaretto Del Garda (Italy)
   White wines:
Premières Côtes de Blaye
Ajaccio
Pouilly-Fumé
Chablis

Other dishes to go with this wine
Lamb's lettuce salad with lardons
   and croutons
Ham and grapefruit salad
Sheep's cheese vol-au-vents
Onion tart
Courgette or leek quiche
Creole-style black pudding
Poultry brochettes
Pork and veal brochettes

The sommelier's selection
Château Bois Malot
Château Brethous
Château Penin

LES BAUX DE PROVENCE ROUGE
tagliatelle bolognese

Flat pasta like tagliatelle goes well with wine, but a tomato-based Bolognese sauce can be a problem. You have the acid tomato flavours to contend with and, just to complicate matters further, there is the deliciously distracting smell of the minced meat.

The real problem with a Bolognese sauce is the notoriously wine-unfriendly taste of tomato. To counteract the acidity, it helps if the sauce has been reduced to a jammy consistency and seasoned with herbs, pepper and a touch of grated Parmesan. Thankfully, the dish also includes pasta - flat, tagliatelle-shaped pasta that works well with wine, unlike spaghetti-type pasta that does not. My favourite is fresh tagliatelle cooked al dente so it remains firm when mixed with the sauce.

The most obvious choice with a dish like this would be an Italian red. Alternatively, we could depart from the Italian theme and take a look at what the Midi has to offer. Some of these wines suggest interesting possibilities – a red Baux de Provence is a good example. This is a dense and richly coloured wine with a fruity edge of red berries plus peppery, almost musky notes that go well with Mediterranean cuisine. Supporting these flavours are unmistakable aromas of the Provencale garrigue. The wine is concentrated and well behaved with a generous, sunny side to its personality. Given an hour to open up in the decanter before serving, a Baux de Provence Rouge will make a delightful addition to any summer dinner.

Other wines to go with this dish

Red wines:

Cabardès

Côtes de Provence

Chianti Classico (Italy)

Valpolicella (Italy)

Montepulciano di Abruzzo (Italy)

Corvo Sicilia (Italy)

Rosé wines:

Côtes de Provence

Les Baux de Provence

Cerasuolo di Abruzzo (Italy)

Other dishes to go with this wine

Purslane salad, with a slice of duck
foie gras

Smoked duck breast fillet, with
vinaigrette made with truffle oil

Marinated sardines

Stuffed vegetables Nice-style

Greek moussaka

Goat's cheeses (Picodon Demi-Sec)

The sommelier's selection

Château Romanin

Domaine Hauvette

Mas Sainte-Berthe

TAVEL
mixed leaves with roasted goat's cheese

AOC
Tavel
REGION
Rhône Valley
ROSE WINE
AREA
950ha
CULTIVARS
Mainly:
Grenache
Syrah
Cinsault
Also:
Clairette
Piquepoul
Calitor
Bourboulenc
Mourvèdre
Carignan

Appearances can be deceiving – this apparently inoffensive little salad of mixed leaves and goat's cheese can go badly wrong with wine. Bitter-tasting leaves with a somewhat acid dressing can easily upset the balance of flavours, despite the soothing presence of the roasted goat's cheese.

Generally speaking, wine and lettuces do not mix. That said, it's important to distinguish between different types of lettuce. Endive lettuce is bitter tasting, garden lettuce (Batavia, Romane) tends to be sweeter, and small-leafed greens such as lamb's lettuce and purslane are sweetest of all. The safest bet with wine is a rich assortment of tender, small-leafed greens such as lamb's lettuce, dandelion, red endive, oakleaf lettuce and purslane. For extra softness, I suggest a dressing made with a trickle of lemon juice (rather than vinegar which I find too aggressive), oil, mixed herbs and a spoonful of poultry stock. Adding the goat's cheese – a semi-dry Crottin or a Picodon Demi-Sec, oven-grilled for a few minutes – will intensify the taste of all the other ingredients. Serve this dish at the end of the meal, and it will do dual duty as salad and cheese course.

However, the goat's cheese is another problem when it comes to choosing the wine. Goat's cheese usually goes best with a white wine – a Sancerre or a Sauvignon de Loire, for instance. But given the mixed leaves, I would be more inclined to serve a rosé that in any case stands a better chance against the somewhat acid dressing. On the other hand, the fruity freshness of the wine must not clash with the acidulous flavours of the salad – so you need a wine with good body and density. A Tavel rosé from the southern Rhône Valley has much to recommend it here – precise aromas of macerated redcurrants, power, well-judged warmth on the palate and generous volume. Not a wine for all occasions by any means, but one with enough roundness and thirst-quenching crispness to make a very sensible choice with this salad. In fact, a Tavel pairs well with a number of 'difficult' dishes, including spicy or sweet-and-sour cuisine. Serve the wine more or less chilled (10-12°C/50-53.6°F) depending on its age and what it is to be served with. With this particular salad, I prefer a youngish wine, served chilled so as to retain its fleshiness and characteristic hint of redcurrants.

Other wines to go with this dish
  Rosé wines:
Gigondas
Côteaux du Languedoc
Vin de Corse Calvi
Sancerre or Chinon
Côtes du Jura 'Corail'
  White wines:
Sancerre
Pouilly-Fumé
Mentou-Salon
Châteauneuf-du-Pape
Vin de Pays d'Oc (Sauvignon-based)

Other dishes to go with this wine
  With a 2-3 year old wine (10°C/50°F):
Salad of mussels and mixed leaves
  with raspberry vinegar
Black pudding Creole-style
Fish terrine
Poultry terrine
Tabouleh (cracked wheat salad)
  With a 4-6 year old wine (12°C/53.6°F):
Roast chicken
Beef satay and other Asian dishes
Pork chop charcutière-style
Goat's or sheep's cheese

The sommelier's selection
Château de Trinquevedel
Domaine de la Mordorée
Domaine Roc de l'Olivet
Domaine Verda

ANJOU-VILLAGES BRISSAC
tomme de brebis (sheep's cheese)

AOC
Anjou-Villages Brissac
REGION
Loire
RED WINE AREA
100ha
CULTIVARS
Mainly:
Cabernet-Franc
Also:
Cabernet-Sauvignon

Contrary to popular opinion, few cheeses go well with tannic red wines. A tomme de brebis is an exception and has what it takes to complement the texture and absorb the power of red wines.

Fancy a drop of red wine with your cheese? If so, you may well be in for a disappointment because in fact a white wine would usually be a wiser choice. The problem is that dense tannins clash with the majority of cheeses, whether hard, washed-rind, goat's or blue cheese. One of the rare exceptions to this rule is a tomme de brébis. It has a fine, melt-in-the-mouth texture that holds out well against powerfully tannic reds – whereas it doesn't go at all with overly tender wines. I particularly like it with an Anjou-Villages Brissac, a wine I discovered quite recently at the Salon des Vins de Loire. I had the privilege of being there a few years ago when Anjou-Villages Brissac was granted appellation status and I have watched its wines develop ever since. It used to be confused with Anjou-Villages, and definitely deserved to become an appellation in its own right. The wines are mainly based on Cabernet-Franc plantings in the Brissac area of Anjou. They tend to be brightly coloured, with fairly persistent notes of black and red fruits and that somewhat vegetal but thirst-quenching quality typical of the Cabernets. They exhibit noticeably more power and density than most Anjou wines, with delicate but assertive tannins that show to perfection alongside a tomme de brebis. Anjou-Villages Brissac only became an appellation in 1998, so it's a bit too early to know whether its wines will age well or not. But if I had to bet on it, I'd say they could easily make it past six or seven.

Other wines to go with a Tomme de brebis
Chinon Rouge
Bourgueil Rouge
Médoc
Saint-Emilion
Irouléguy Rouge
Cahors
Bergerac Rouge
Pécharmant
Buzet Rouge

Other dishes to go with this wine
Charcuterie platter
Thick grilled beefsteak
Roast leg of lamb
Lamb stew
Venison in French brown sauce

The sommelier's selection
Château de Montgueret
Domaine de Montgilet
Domaine des Bonnes Gagnes
Domaine des Charbotières
Domaine des Rochelles

CIDRE DRY
roast camembert with apples

The emblematic Camembert, possibly the most famous cheese in the world, is inseparable from baguette and a glass of red wine. It is one of those things that were once the symbols of French national identity. The truth is, Camembert is very difficult to combine with a red wine because it makes the wine seem hard and bitter-tasting ...

Contrary to popular opinion, Camembert does not go especially well with red wine, and the same is true for any ripened white-mould cheese. You stand a better chance with a smooth, acid white but the result will never be that great. One way around the problem is to be creative with the cheese itself. In this recipe, for instance, the Camembert is stripped of its rind and warmed in the oven. A light cooking highlights the creaminess of the cheese but will inevitably brings out its irresistible, powerfully fragrant lactic taste – which you have to play down with the right accompaniment. Serving Camembert with baked apples – roasted apple rings or thin, oven-dried apple slices – thankfully allows us to create a combination based on fruitiness. What we need with this dish is an apple-tasting drink, so what better than cider?

Cider's delicate effervescence has just the airy touch required with such a pungently aromatic dish – and its fruity apple nose will go perfectly with the raw milk and silage smells in the cheese. For me, this dish and a dry cider (which always retains some sweetness) form a logical combination of two terroir products that share the same fruit flavours. It strikes a perfect balance between the aromatic freshness of the cider and the power of the Camembert.

Other dishes to go with cider
    With a dry cider:
Chicory salad with apple cubes
    and raisins
Pays d'Auge poultry in a cream and cider
    sauce with white rice
Rabbit in cider
Buckwheat pancakes (with white ham,
    Gruyère cheese)
Andouillette in cider sauce
    With a sweet cider:
Apple-based desserts: apple tart,
caramelised upside-down apple tart
    (tarte Tatin), apple granita, baked
    apples with sugar and vanilla ice-cream
Pear-based desserts: pear tart, tarte
Bourdaloue with almonds, pear charlotte
    with custard
Candied fruit diplomat
Sweet pancakes with fruits or flambé
    (avoid chocolate)
Baked Alaska with vanilla praline

Wines to go with this dish
Brut Champagne
Saumur Brut
Cava (sparkling wine from Catalonia,
    Spain)
Asti Spumante Secco (Italy)

The sommelier's selection
Le Père Jules
Château de Hauteville
Domaine Louis Dupont
Les Vergers du Pays d'Auge
Manoir La Brière des Fontaines
Christian Drouin SA

CHAMPAGNE ROSE

langres cheese vol-au-vents

AOC
Champagne
REGION
Champagne
SPARKLING
ROSE WINE
This AOC also
produces dry and
moelleux
sparking whites
AREA
Total 31,000ha
for the AOC
as a whole
CULTIVARS
Pinot Noir
Pinot Meunier
Chardonnay

The appeal of this recipe lies in the contrast between the hot, crispy, golden, freshly baked puff pastry and the warm, creamy, melt-in-the-mouth cheese, served stripped of its rind, straight from the oven. Suitably prepared like this, a strong-flavoured Langres cheese might well lend itself to wine …

Generally speaking, a pungently aromatic Langres cheese is unfriendly to wine, making red wine in particular seem hard, bitter and metallic. This ingeniously presented vol-au-vent plays on the contrast between the notes of freshly baked puff pastry and the measured flavour of the cheese. Texture, taste and temperature are minutely calculated to pair with the wine. The truth is that my starting point for this combination was the Champagne, rather than the dish. As a sommelier, I have often had to devise creative ways of featuring Champagne from the first course to the last. The problem of course is the sheer variety of Champagnes – rosé, Blanc de Blancs, Blanc de Noirs, Brut and non-Brut. Then again, such an embarrassment of choice does open up a wealth of possibilities. For this vol-au-vent filled with Langres cheese, the choice has to be a rosé Champagne. Its delicate bubbles will add a very welcome thirst-quenching quality and it has a particularly persistent palate thanks to dense texture (from the Pinot Noir) and those aromas of redcurrants and greengages typical of a rosé. A rosé Champagne is thus more likely to stand up gently but firmly to the strong-flavoured cheese. Serve the Champagne chilled (around 10°C/50°F – not so cold as to jar with the hot vol-au-vent). This will bring out its volume and save it from seeming mean alongside the mighty Langres.

Other dishes to go with rosé Champagne
Shrimp salad flavoured with paprika
Peeled, warm king prawns in paprika sauce
Pikeperch or pike roast in a meat gravy
Grilled red mullet with rouille sauce
Bouillabaisse
Cheeses: tomme de brebis, dry or
    medium-dry goat's cheese
    (not ash-coated varieties)
Red fruit mousse
Raspberry iced bombe
Fraisier (strawberry gateau)
Red fruit gratin

Other wines to go with this dish
Crémant de Loire Rosé
Marsannay Rosé
Tavel
Bandol Rosé

The sommelier's selection
Billecart-Salmon
Bollinger
Deutz
Gosset
Krug
Taittinger
Perrier Jouet

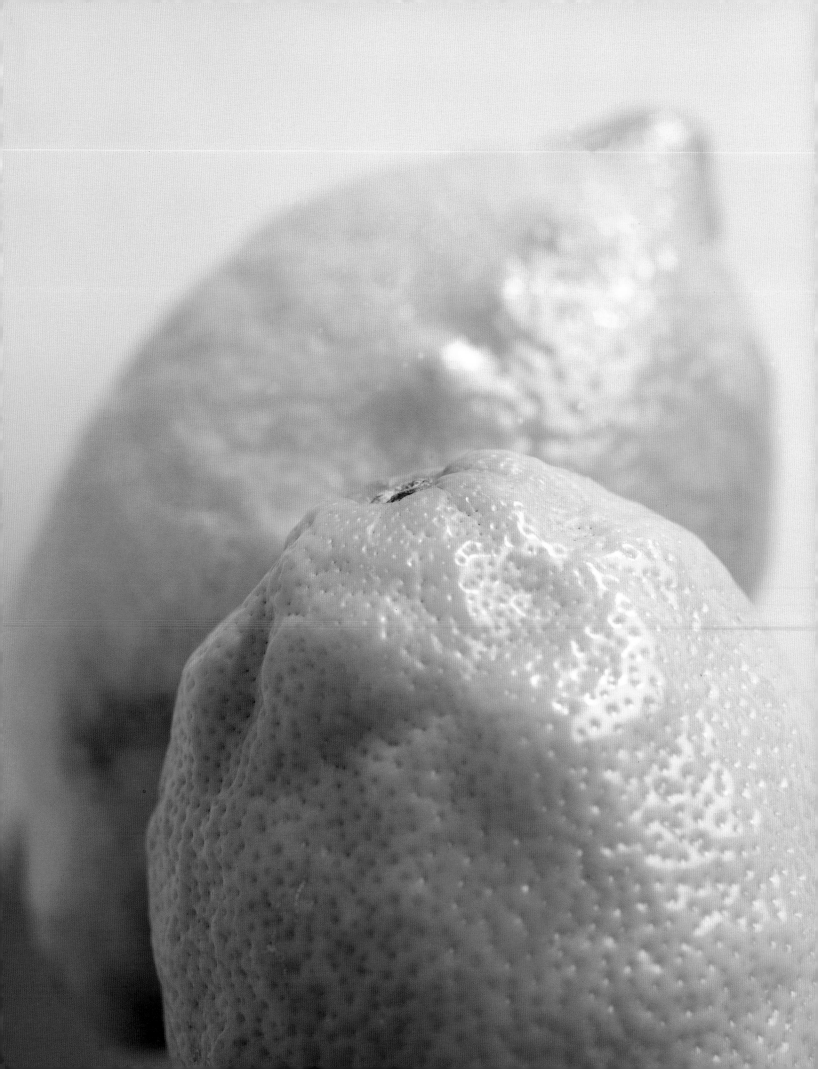

SAUTERNES
pear and roquefort tart

AOC
Sauternes
REGION
Bordeaux
LIQUOREUX
WHITE WINE
AREA
1,650ha
CULTIVARS
Mainly:
Sémillon
Also:
Sauvignon
Muscadelle

This ingenious, highly original tart is a pudding and cheese course rolled into one – as much a 'savoury dessert' as a 'warm sweet starter'. The contrasting flavours of the fruit, cheese and flaky pastry give it a wonderfully complex range of aromas.

This delicious tart is a real treat, with its complex blend of fine, crispy crust and barely cooked pear slices, sprinkled with sugar and thin slivers of Roquefort. The cheese is added at the last moment so as to melt into the gaps left by the pear slices as they shrink in cooking. The result is a triumph of smoothness and delicacy, especially if made with juicy pears that will remain crisp once cooked. On the palate, the granular flesh of the fruit merges with the fragrant, melt-in-the-mouth creaminess of the molten Roquefort. Such a lavishly aromatic dish deserves a wine of similar calibre – one with expressive characteristics that complement the naturally acidulous flavours of the tart, but enough voluminous texture to stand up to the smoothness of the dish.

There is really only one choice here, and that is a Sauternes. Other sweet wines would do of course, but very few are so intimately suited to pear and Roquefort tart. In fact, it was in the Sauternes region that I first discovered this irresistibly delectable dessert. I love the balance of the great Sauternes, that combination of full-bodied Sauvignon aromas and dense Sémillon texture with just a touch of fantasy from the Muscadelle. But such supremely refined wines cannot be paired with just any dish. These are powerful, full-bodied wines for special occasions, with that heady complexity that comes from candied, honeyed notes and hints of cinnamon, caramel and citrus. A Sauternes is some 10 years in the making, but the wait is well worth it. A common mistake is to serve it with sweet desserts – a sickly combination that is definitely best avoided. What it goes best with in fact are complex and quite spicy flavours, such as mild curries or sauces flavoured with saffron or ginger; also blue cheese, like the Roquefort in this tart. I like to decant the wine so as to admire its golden tones, serving it no colder than 10°C (50°F). What you get then is a wine that fully expresses its sweetness, with an intensity and elegance to die for.

Other dishes to go with this wine
With a wine less than 10 years old:
Foie gras on toast
Small, saffron-flavoured cheese puffs
Roast lobster in citrus sauce
Roquefort and other blue cheeses
Exotic fruit salad, with chestnut ice-cream
    and ginger lace biscuits
Dried fruit diplomat and gingerbread
Pithiviers (puff pastry with frangipane filling)
With a wine more than 10 years old:
Veal sweetbreads with morel mushrooms
Medallions of veal in Sauternes and
    truffle sauce
Roast free-range poultry with
    crystallised lemon

Other wines to go with this dish
Barsac
Cadillac
Loupiac
Sainte-Croix-du-Mont
Pacherenc du Vic-Bilh Moelleux
Alsace Riesling Sélection de Grains Nobles
Vouvray Moelleux
Botrytis Sémillon, from Victoria (Australia)
Vin de Constance (South Africa)

The sommelier's selection
Château Raymond-Lafon
Château de Rayne Vigneau
Château d'Yquem
Château Gillette
Château Lafaurie-Peyraguey
Château Rieussec
    Barsac:
Château Climens
Château Doisy Daëne
Château Nairac

ALSACE GEWURZTRAMINER VENDANGES TARDIVES

apple tart with a hint of lemon

AOC
Alsace Gewurztraminer
REGION
Alsace
WHITE WINE
VENDANGES TARDIVES
This AOC mainly produces dry whites
AREA
2,500ha
CULTIVAR
Gewurztraminer

The success of this tart depends on a subtle balance of sweetness and acidity. The touch of lemon adds character to the dish but not at the expense of the apple flavours. The wine must show the same discretion, contributing to the harmony without overdoing the sweetness.

You need really crisp sweet apples for this tart. My favourites are Royal Gala, Queen of the Pippins and Reinettes Clochard that all hold up well when cooked. I usually rub them with lemon before arranging them over the short-crust pastry base. This gives the tart just the right amount of citrus tang – noticeable but never excessive. I also halve the apples, as for a tarte Tatin (upside-down apple tart), rather than slice them. Thicker fruit cooks more slowly, gradually developing that soft texture needed for this dish. All you need then is a knob of butter and a sprinkling of sugar just before baking. For a more acidulous taste, simply add some grated lemon peel when you are about to serve.

As to the wine, anything overly sweet would be too sickly with this tart. That's why I would choose an Alsace Gewurztraminer Vendanges Tardives. This is a wine with a magnificent, captivating bouquet of exotic fruits (litchi, mango, papaya), candied citrus and roses. Its spicy notes – to which it owes the name 'gewurtz' – give it a thoroughbred quality. Its density of sweetness calls for a slightly acidulous dessert that will allow it to express its full range of aromas. The wine should open on the palate with a smooth attack, followed by a return to tangible sweetness, then an immediate sensation of crispness that will be highlighted by the flavours of the apple tart. Wine and dessert are in perfect harmony – especially if you chill the wine to 8-9°C (46.4-48.2°F) so as to bring out its exquisitely refined, almost crunchy notes of fragrant fruit.

Other dishes to go with this wine
Sautéed semi-cooked Alsace duck
    foie gras with cooked apples, mangos
    and white pepper
Fourme d'Ambert, Bleu de Bresse, Munster
Mango tart
Lemon tart
Litchi soup
Exotic fruit sorbet
Pear sorbet
Frozen pear charlotte
Mango vacherin (meringue cake with mangos)

Other wines to go with this dish
Jurançon Moelleux
Pacherenc du Vic-Bilh Moelleux
Alsace Muscat Vendanges Tardives
Vins de Loire Moelleux: Jasnières,
    Anjou-Côteaux de la Loire,
    Montlouis, Vouvray

The sommelier's selection
Cave de Pfaffenheim
Domaine Blanck et Fils
Domaine Seppi Landemann

BONNEZEAUX
yellow plum tart

AOC
Bonnezeaux
REGION
Loire
VIN BLANC
LIQUOREUX
AREA
120ha
CULTIVAR
Chenin

I am particular fond of this tart with its lovely saffron tones, the quite thick texture of the plum skin contrasting with the softness of the cooked flesh. But beware – such a characterful dessert needs a wine with good length.

Making a really good yellow plum tart isn't easy. The short crust pastry for instance must not become soaked in juice, and the bed of confectioner's custard under the plums must not be so sweet as to mask the plums' natural acidity. Ideally this dessert should be served with a sweet white wine (Blanc Liquoreux), one packed with sweetness but ending with a good, fresh finish. That argues for a Bonnezeaux. Its aromas of stoned fruits, honey and minerals will combine beautifully with those masterful flavours of patisserie, fruit and vanilla in a cold yellow plum tart. The Bonnezeaux appellation, which recently celebrated its fiftieth anniversary, is a great favourite of mine. Yellow plum tart is often served with a white eau-de-vie but, for me, a Bonnezeaux is far more original. What you have then is a dynamic, entirely complementary combination that plays to its strengths: scents of fruit echoed in the dish and the wine, honeyed aromas, dense sweetness, sumptuous fragrance and lots of mineral freshness. The textures on the palate are deliciously harmonious, the wine's viscosity serving as the link between the smoothness of the cream and the juicy melt-in-the-mouth fruit. The aromas combine but never collide, bringing the meal to an end on a delightfully thirst-quenching note. Note that a Bonnezeaux is quite capable of aging. I recently tasted a 50 year old wine that left me positively entranced!

Other dishes to go with this wine
Terrine of duck foie gras
Supreme of farm hen with foie gras
Melted Roquefort or Chabichou cheese
   on toast, mature Saint-Marcellin cheese
Exotic fruit salad
Exotic fruit tart
Exotic fruit zabaglione with zest of citrus
Melon soup with coriander seeds
Vanilla crème brulée
Vanilla, toffee, praline or exotic fruit
   ice-cream (not red berries, coffee
   or chocolate)

Other wines to go with this dish
   Moelleux or liquoreux wines:
Côteaux de l'Aubance
Alsace Tokay-Pinot Gris, Sélection de
   Grains Nobles
   Vins Doux Naturels:
Muscat de Beaumes-de-Venise
   Eaux-de-vie:
Mirabelle de Lorraine
Quetsche
Prune

The sommelier's selection
Château de Fesles
Domaine de Terre Brune
Domaine des Gagneries
Domaine des Petits Quarts
Domaine René Renou

MUSCAT DU CAP CORSE
lemon meringue pie

An ordinary lemon tart is definitely not an easy dessert to combine with a wine. The contrast of textures is extreme – firm, shortbread dough and soft filling – and the tang of lemon almost stuns the taste buds. Adding the meringue makes things a bit easier.

The problem with an ordinary lemon tart is the tartness of the citrus flavour. This otherwise refined and delicious dessert has a persistently sharp taste that could have disastrous consequences for the wine that goes with it. Adding a light meringue topping helps to buffer the lemony aromas and makes enough of a difference to affect our choice of wine. Essentially, what we need here is a powerfully aromatic wine with a viscous texture that recalls the creaminess of the lemon filling. The majority of Muscat-based Vins Doux Naturels (VDN) have precisely those qualities. These are naturally sweet wines, made by a process that halts fermentation through the addition of grape spirit. The wine remains rich in fruit sugars that have not been consumed by the yeasts.

My preference with a lemon meringue pie is a Muscat du Cap Corse. It has all the smoothness and alcoholic presence to be expected of the VDN, but is distinguished by its pronounced notes of citrus. This elegant fruitiness, that echoes the notes in the pie, serves to temper the acidulous freshness of the lemon filling. The result is a combination of near-perfect harmony, a merging of wine and dish, with no loss of soul. Their viscosity fades on the palate, the pie melting in the mouth as the wine liquefies in the heat. The crunchy shortbread dough and velvety meringue add their own different textures, creating a subtle alliance that I find quite irresistible. An ordinary lemon tart is certainly not to be sniffed at, mind you. But the flavours are so uncannily intense and the taste so strong that you would need a rather more robust style of Vin Doux Naturel.

Other wines to go with this dish
With lemon meringue pie:
Muscat de Beaumes-de-Venise
Muscat de Mireval
Muscat de Frontignan
Muscat de Lunel
Malvasia delle Lipari (Italy)
Moscato di Pantelleria (Italy)
Alsace Gewurztraminer Vendanges
    Tardives
Côtes du Jura Vin de Paille
    With an ordinary lemon tart:
Muscat de Rivesaltes
Muscat de Saint-Jean-de-Minervois

Other dishes to go with this wine
Raw foie gras with coarse sea salt
Blue cheeses
Other citrus tarts: citron, orange,
    grapefruit
Grand-Marnier soufflé

The sommelier's selection
Clos Nicrosi
Domaine Arena
Domaine Gentile
Domaine Leccia
Domaine Pierretti

COTES DU JURA VIN DE PAILLE
crystallised orange peel coated in black chocolate

AOC
Côtes du Jura
REGION
Jura
VIN LIQUOREUX
AREA
619ha
CULTIVARS
Mainly:
Savagnin
Also:
Chardonnay
Poulsard
Trousseau
Pinot Noir

These exquisite chocolaty-orange confections are eaten like a sweet, with your fingers. They are more of an indulgence than a dessert, made for after dinner conversations when you can linger over every last delectable bite – before reaching for another.

These delicious sweets, known in French as 'orangettes' (little oranges) or 'sarments de vigne' (vine shoots, because of their twisted shape), are by no means easy to pair with wine. You have to reckon with the bitterness of plain chocolate and notes of roasted cocoa; also the fairly rugged acid tones and touch of candied orange peel, plus the mix of soft and crispy textures. A challenging confection to say the least, but we can at least rule out an overly tender wine. The persistency of the orange peel calls for a wine with bags of personality, plenty of length on the palate and decent sweetness. I can think of few suitable candidates apart from some of the more robust Vins Doux Naturels.

Personally, I fancy a more complex sort of harmony in this case, one that veers away from the idea of sweetness towards a rarer combination altogether. What we need here is a Vin de Paille du Jura. One word would sum up this wine: indomitable. Even the way it is made is original. The grapes (red and white) are laid out to dry for two months on 'claies' (mats or racks) that were traditionally made of straw. Drying the berries concentrates the sugars in the wines, leading to a long fermentation period. As it develops, a Vin de Paille takes on characteristically nutty, almost oxidized notes. It is generally bottled in half-bottles and should be savoured slowly, as an indulgence in itself. For that reason, it makes an ideal match for crystallised orange peel. Otherwise, this interesting wine with its high sugar and alcohol concentrations and notes of candied citrus, apple and spices is not an easy wine to pair with food. For me, there is an almost meditative quality about a Vin de Paille. It's a wine to be sipped as you linger around the table after a really good meal, putting the world to rights. The key to enjoying this unconventional combination is to take your time, a nibble here, a sip there. A sensual experience if ever there was one …

Other wines to go with this dish
Banyuls
Maury
Rasteau
Mavrodaphne Patras (Greece)
Tawny Port
Madeira Malvasia

Other dishes to go with this wine
Cheeses: Picodon with raisins and
honey bread
Floating island pudding

The sommelier's selection
Château d'Arlay
Domaine Badoz
Domaine Rousselot Pailley
Domaine Labet Père et Fils

BANYULS
plain chocolate fondant

A chocolate fondant is full of surprises. Firm, almost crispy on the outside and deliciously smooth on the inside, it reveals a variety of chocolaty characteristics. This classical, intense-tasting dessert goes well with an Arabica sauce or a garnish of glacé cherries.

Plain chocolate has inspired a great many traditional French desserts but it has never been easy to combine with wine. Its bitterness and pungently roasted notes get in the way of most combinations; not many drinks can stand up to chocolate without overpowering it. Combinations that have been shown to work are chocolate with old rums, marc or raspberry eau-de-vie. What it most definitely does not go with are the very sweet Vins Liquoreux Blancs that tend to pale into insignificance alongside the wicked intensity of chocolate. The best match for plain chocolate remains a Vin Doux Naturel. When accompanying a chocolate fondant and Morello cherries, this is a wine that will overcome the bitterness of the chocolate but conserve the aromas of fruit in eau de vie. The wine's own candied and roasted notes complete the impression of harmony.

Banyuls and plain chocolate go back a long way. This naturally sweet wine comes from the extreme south of France, close to the Spanish border. A vineyard kissed by Mediterranean sea spray gives Banyuls a mineral energy and almost iodised taste that make it an ideal companion for certain types of roasted crustacean. To this day, I am filled with emotion at the memory of the roast lobster in Banyuls I once tasted at Jean Bardet's restaurant ... The eau-de-vie used in the making of Banyuls cools down its kirsch-like aromas and dense, compelling sweetness, making this a very digestible wine. A real lesson in pleasure - providing you don't drink too much of it of course. There are various styles of Banyuls to choose from. For a plain chocolate fondant with coffee cream, I would pick a more mature, rancio style of Banyuls. But with a red fruit garnish (such as Morello cherries) I would choose a younger, 2-3 year old vintage with aromas of fruit liqueur more closely resembling those in the garnish. Whatever your choice, Banyuls is always exceptional. It is usually best decanted, partly to remove the lees, but also to show off its magnificent tones that range from amber to glossy terracotta.

Other dishes to go with this wine
Foie gras terrine
Roast lobster in Banyuls wine
Roast pheasant in Banyuls wine
Roquefort and other blue cheeses
Plain chocolate mousse
Caramel custard dessert
Prunes in wine
Prune tart
Tiramisu

Other wines to go with this dish
Maury
Rasteau
Porto

The sommelier's selection
Cave l'Étoile
Domaine de la Rectorie
Domaine Mas Blanc
Domaine Vial-Magnères

MUSCAT DE MIREVAL
exotic fruit sorbet

AOC
Muscat de Mireval
REGION
Languedoc
VIN DOUX NATUREL
AREA
260ha
CULTIVAR
Muscat à Petits Grains

The acidulous flavours of an exotic fruit sorbet, made with mangos, pineapple, bananas or even mandarins, make this a pleasingly refreshing finish to any meal. To offset the sorbet's watery nature, I like to add a touch of crispiness with an almond and citrus lace biscuit.

A really refreshing dessert is a welcome end to any meal, especially a heavy one. A barely sweet sorbet, made from just water and fruit, always seems cool and light but it does need the added sweetness of a wine accompaniment. The only really satisfactory match is a wine that has plenty of up-front fruit – so what better than a Muscat? These are wines made by a process of fortification that stops fermentation, so leaving the fresh grape flavours intact. A Muscat de Mireval will provide an easy harmony here. Based on the Muscat à Petits Grains cultivar, Muscat de Mireval comes from a small appellation near Montpellier. It has all the fruit and concentrated sweetness needed to pair with a sorbet. But it is also quite tender, with a taste like biting into deliciously fresh grapes. That pure fruit flavour, supported by refined alcohol, serves to reveal the other aromas. But it would be too much to serve such a wine with an overly sweet dessert. For an exotic fruit sorbet, I like a young, 1-2 year old Muscat de Mireval, served well chilled (7-8°C/44.8-46.4°F) so as not to seem warm alongside the iced dessert. But these original wines also age well, developing spicier, more candied notes that make them a splendid accompaniment to some savoury dishes.

Other wines to go with this dish
Barsac
Loupiac
Sainte-Croix-du-Mont
Alsace Muscat Sélection de Grains Nobles
Alsace Gewurztraminer
Alsace Riesling
Vino Santo Toscano (Italy)
Trockenbeerenauslese (Germany)
Eiswein (ice wine) from the Moselle or the
   Palatinate (Germany)
Niagara Icewine (Canada)

Other dishes to go with this wine
Duck with peaches
Foie gras and figs or dried apricots,
   almond bread
Cheeses: dry Pélardon des Cévennes
   with olive oil
Crystallised citrus fruit
Crème brulée with ginger
Caramel custard dessert
Frozen nougat
Tiramisu

The sommelier's selection
Domaine de la Capelle
Domaine du Moulinas
Domaine du Mas Neuf

Andouillette with thick-cut chips, p100

Six andouillette '5A'

Glass white wine (a nice little Chablis,
for instance)

Olive oil, 1 onion, pepper

Oil the sausages and arrange them on a bed of finely chopped onions, and place in a very hot oven for 15-20 minutes. Turn the sausages over several times, moistening with the white wine at regular intervals. The onions should meanwhile caramelise in the sausage juices. Add pepper, but no salt. Serve the sausages with thick-cut chips, fried golden brown on the outside but with a rich potato taste on the inside.

Apple tart with a hint of lemon, p140

1 sheet ready-rolled short-crust pastry dough

6 Royal Gala or Rennet apples

Half lemon

1 tbsp sugar

Butter to grease the flan case

Line a greased flan case with the pastry. Peel the apples, rub them with the lemon juice then cut them into quarters. Arrange the apples in a rosette shape over the pastry base, sprinkle with sugar and dot with small pieces of butter. Bake in a hot oven for 30 minutes (180°C/355°F, Gas Mark 7). Just before serving, sprinkle with grated lemon peel.

Bay-leaf flavoured John Dory with courgettes, p60

6 John Dory fillets

12 bay leaves, 3 tbsp olive oil

3 courgettes, 1 clove garlic

Coarse sea salt, freshly milled pepper

With a paring knife, slice the courgettes into thin strips, then brown them in a frying pan with the crushed garlic and a drizzle of olive oil. Season lightly with salt and keep warm. Using a pointed knife, insert the bay leaves between the skin and flesh of each fillet. Then lay them skin-side down in a hot frying pan lightly greased with olive oil. Cook for five minutes on one side and roughly 6-7 minutes on the other.

Transfer the fish to warm plates, placing each fillet on a thin bed of courgette strips. Serve immediately, drizzled with olive oil and sprinkled with coarse sea salt.

Beaufort soufflé, p32

1-2oz (40g) butter, 1-2oz (40g) flour

14fl oz ((400ml) milk

5 egg yolks, 6 egg whites

1oz (20g) butter

4oz (100g) grated Beaufort cheese

Nutmeg, salt, pepper

Make a béchamel sauce with the butter, the flour and the milk. Season with salt and pepper and add some grated nutmeg. Stir in the Beaufort cheese and the egg yolks then fold in the stiffly beaten egg whites. Pour the mixture into a buttered and floured soufflé dish, 8 inches (20cm) in diameter. Bake in a hot oven for 30 minutes (170°C/340°F, Gas Mark 6).

Beef Wellington with mushrooms, artichokes and blackcurrant juice, p90

2lb 12oz (1.2kg) fillet of beef

6 artichoke bases cooked and ready prepared

7oz (200g) mushrooms (or 1-2oz/40g truffles)

1 clove garlic, 1 beaten egg, 2oz (50g) butter

1 sheet ready-prepared flaky pastry

Salt, pepper

FOR THE SAUCE:

8fl oz (200ml) meat juices

2 tbsp blackcurrants (fresh or canned)

1oz (25g) butter

Fine-chop the artichoke bases and sauté in butter with just a pinch of garlic. Fry the sliced mushrooms in a knob of butter. Then brown the fillet of beef on all sides in a frying pan and set aside to cool in the refrigerator.

Roll out the flaky pastry, then spread with a layer of artichoke slices, placing the fillet of beef on top and sprinkling with the mushrooms (or truffles). Fold the edges of the pastry over the meat and brush with beaten egg. Pre-heat the oven to 170°C/340°F, Gas Mark 6.

To make the sauce: Re-heat the meat juices and adjust the seasoning. Add the blackcurrants and thicken the sauce with the fresh butter, beating in a knob at a time. Set aside and keep warm.

Raise the oven temperature to 190°C/375°F, Gas Mark 8, and cook the beef Wellington for 10 minutes, followed by 15 minutes at 180°C/355°F, Gas Mark 7. Remove the meat

and leave it to relax for five minutes before slicing. Serve immediately.

Blanquette de veau (veal stew) old-fashioned style, p96

3lb 8oz (1.5kg) shoulder of veal cut into
large cubes

1 carrot, 1 leek, 1 onion stuck with a clove,
half lemon

1 bouquet garni (parsley stalks, thyme, bay leaf,
celery)

3oz (75g) flour, 3oz (75g) butter

7oz (200g) small onions

7oz (200g) mushrooms

7fl oz (200ml) fresh cream

Sugar, salt, pepper

Place the meat in a large saucepan and cover with cold water. Bring to the boil, skim and cook for five minutes. Add the vegetables and the bouquet garni, and simmer for 40-45 minutes. Meanwhile wipe and shred the mushrooms, and cook them in water and lemon juice. Cook the onions in a saucepan with a knob of butter, a pinch of sugar and salt.

Make a roux with the butter and flour. When the meat is cooked, take two and a half pints (1.5l) of the meat stock and add to the roux. Bring to the boil and cook for 10 minutes, then add the cream. Lift out the meat with a slotted spoon, place it in the sauce with the mushrooms and onions and leave to simmer for about 10 minutes. Just before serving, add a few drops of lemon juice to sharpen the flavour. For a richer sauce, stir in a tablespoon of fresh cream mixed with an egg yoke, but on no account let the mixture boil.

Bresse chicken with St George's mushrooms, p76

1 Blue Foot Bresse chicken (renowned for its
white meat)

2oz (50g) butter, 4fl oz (100ml) chicken stock

1lb 12oz (800g) St George's mushrooms

2 shallots, 3 sprigs chives, salt, pepper

Gut, season and truss the chicken, setting aside the fat removed from the body cavity. Cut this into small pieces and heat with half the butter in a casserole. Now place the chicken in the casserole, breast side down,

Quantities for six people

and brown it first on the breast then on the other side. Transfer it to a hot oven (180°C/355°F, Gas Mark 7) and roast for about an hour, basting regularly with the cooking juices. Meanwhile, rinse and drain the St George's mushrooms. Then sweat them in a saucepan over a low heat with a little butter for five minutes. Drain the mushrooms (setting aside the cooking liquid) then sauté them with a pinch of the shallots. Remove the chicken from the casserole, discard excess fat and de-glaze the casserole with the mushroom cooking juices and the chicken stock. Reduce the juices and season to taste. Carve the chicken and serve on a bed of St George's mushrooms, coated with the sauce and sprinkled with chives.

Chicken liver terrine, p18

1lb (500g) chicken livers

14oz (400g) loin of pork

1 clove garlic, 1 shallot, 1 bunch parsley

1 egg

1 pinch allspice, 1 pinch ground coriander

2 tsp (1/4oz) salt, pinch of pepper

4fl oz (100ml) port

Caul fat

Chop the meat, using the food processor's fine shredding disc for the pork and the coarse shredder for the chicken livers. Mince the garlic with the peeled shallots. Chop and rinse the parsley.

Combine the meats in a mixing bowl with the salt, pepper, allspice and coriander. Add the garlic plus one tablespoon shallots, two tablespoons parsley, the egg and the port. Press the complete mixture into a terrine dish and cover with the rinsed and drained caul fat, tucking it well in around the edges. Refrigerate for approximately six hours.

Pre-heat the oven to 150°C/300°F, Gas Mark 3. Cover the terrine and place it in a roasting pan, pouring in hot water to a level about two-thirds up the side of the dish. Cook in a hot oven for an hour and a half, then leave the terrine to stand for 15 minutes at room temperature. While it cools, cut out a piece of cardboard to fit inside the top of the terrine and wrap it in tinfoil. Place the cardboard on top of the terrine, weight it heavily (with a tin of vegetables, for instance) then leave it

for three hours in the refrigerator until set. It will keep for up to a week.

Chicken pot-au-feu, p78

3lb (1.3kg) free-range chicken

Assortment of spring vegetables: baby carrots, turnips with tops, young leeks, celery sticks, parsnips

1 onion stuck with a clove, 2 cloves garlic

1 glass dry white wine, 1 bouquet garni

8fl oz (200ml) fresh cream

Salt, peppercorns

Place the chicken in a large stewing pot. Cover with water, bring to the boil and skim well. Add the white wine, the onion, the bouquet garni, the garlic and a few peppercorns. Season with salt and cook for 30 minutes then add the vegetables and continue cooking for a further 15 minutes. Remove the chicken, carve it and arrange it on a serving dish surrounded by the drained vegetables. Make a sauce by reducing a little of the stock with the cream. Adjust the seasoning, then pour it over the chicken and serve immediately.

Comté cheese and walnut pie, p30

2 sheets ready-rolled flaky pastry dough

18fl oz (500ml) milk

4oz (100g) butter, 4oz (100g) flour

4oz (100g) Comté cheese (sliced)

1-2oz (40g) broken walnuts, 1 egg

Salt, pepper and grated nutmeg (pinch each)

Line a buttered pie dish with one sheet of pastry dough. Make a roux with the butter and flour. Then, keeping the pan on the heat, gradually add the hot milk, whisking continuously until the sauce thickens. Then add the sliced cheese, walnuts and seasonings (salt, pepper and nutmeg) and pour into the prepared pastry case. Cover with the second sheet of dough, brush with beaten egg and cook for 40 minutes in a moderate oven, preheated to 170°C/340°F, Gas Mark 6.

Crayfish in aromatic broth, p46

2lb 12oz (1kg) crayfish (approx 20-25 medium-sized crayfish, preferably Red Claw)

2oz (50g) butter for the sauce

FOR THE BROTH:

1pt 15fl oz (1 litre) good dry white wine (preferably Mâcon or Pouilly-Fuissé)

18fl oz (0.5l) water

2 large sweet carrots

1 onion stuck with a clove, 1 shallot

1 peeled lemon with pith removed

Half bay leaf, 1 sprig thyme, 1 clove garlic, small bunch parsley

3 tbsp (40g) coarse sea salt

20 coarsely ground peppercorns

Combine all the ingredients for the aromatic broth and simmer gently for around 30 minutes. Leave to cool.

When you are ready to cook the crayfish, bring the broth back to the boil. Meanwhile, de-vein the crayfish (remove the dark vein from the tail meat by twisting and pulling the middle flipper of the tail).

Plunge the crayfish into the boiling broth and, once the liquid returns to the boil, cook for three minutes. Remove the pan from the heat and leave the crayfish to cool in the broth. Then remove them with a slotted spoon and transfer to a serving dish. Thicken the broth by whisking in the butter, one knob at a time. Adjust the seasoning, strain the sauce through a fine sieve and pour over the crayfish.

Crispy bass in a potato millefeuille topped with foie gras, p64

Six small, 4oz (120g) bass escalopes

Six escalopes fresh foie gras

7oz (200g) Charlotte potatoes

7fl oz (200ml) tomato coulis

2oz (50g) melted butter, 4oz (100g) butter

Salt, pepper

Grate the potatoes and make into small patties. Heat the butter in a non-stick frying pan, then sauté the patties until golden brown on both sides. Remove them from the pan and set aside. In the same pan, sauté the fish, season to taste, set aside and keep warm.

Bring the tomato coulis to the boil then combine with the butter, stirring well to obtain a creamy, slightly foamy sauce.

At the last minute, lightly brown the escalopes of foie gras.

To construct the potato millefeuille: sandwich one bass escalope between two potato patties and top with an escalope of foie gras. Place the millefeuilles on individual plates,

Quantities for six people

surround each with a ribbon of the tomato sauce and serve immediately.

Crystallised orange peel coated in black chocolate, p146

6 twists crystallised orange peel

8oz (200g) very dark plain chocolate

Baking parchment

Cut the orange peel into strips.

Break up the chocolate, place in a bowl, cover with cling film and melt in a double boiler or in the microwave.

Dip the strips of orange peel into the melted chocolate, then place them carefully on a baking tray covered with baking parchment. Leave to cool. Enjoy!

Curry-flavoured shrimp risotto, p122

9oz (250g) Italian Arborio or Carnaroli rice

2fl oz (50ml) oil, 1 glass white wine

1 onion (finely chopped)

6 large shrimps

2oz (50g) grated Parmesan, 1oz (25g) butter

10-11fl oz (300ml) fish stock

1 tsp curry powder, salt, pepper

Sauté the onion in a frying pan with the oil until it starts to brown. Add the rice and mix well until all the grains are evenly coated and glistening. Stir in a glass of white wine plus a little stock. Cook over a very low heat, stirring continuously. Add stock at intervals so as to maintain the liquid at the level of the rice, but no higher. When the grains are tender but still firm (al dente), add the butter a little at a time, then the curry powder, stirring well with a spatula.

Lastly add the grated Parmesan cheese, seasonings and the peeled shrimps. Serve immediately.

Daube de bœuf (beef stew) Provençale-style with black olives, p92

3lb (1.2kg) chuck and silverside of beef, cut into large cubes

1pt 15fl oz (1 litre) red wine

2fl oz (50ml) brandy

1 carrot chopped, 2 onions

1 bouquet garni (thyme, bay leaf, rosemary, celery)

2fl oz (50ml) oil

11oz (300g) tomatoes, 10 cloves garlic

4oz (100g) black olives, salt, peppercorns

1 pork rind

Marinate the meat with the red wine, brandy, carrot, onions, bouquet garni, garlic and peppercorns. Add a trickle of olive oil and leave in the refrigerator overnight.

The next day, drain the beef and sauté with a little of the oil in a large casserole. Add the vegetables and set aside. Bring the marinade to the boil in a saucepan and skim off any scum. Place the pork rind at the bottom of the casserole with the meat and vegetables on top. Pour in the marinade, then add the chopped tomatoes and season with salt. Cover and bake in a very slow oven for three hours, or for two hours in a hot oven (180°C/355°F, Gas Mark 7). Remove the bouquet garni before serving and add the olives.

This sort of stew tastes much better reheated, so prepare it a day in advance.

Duck foie gras cooked in a terrine, p22

One duck liver (about 1lb 4oz/600g)

1 tsp (6g) salt, scant tsp (2g) sugar

Pinch pepper (0.5g), pinch mixed spice (0.5g)

Dash armagnac, dash white port

Freshly milled pepper

Weigh out the seasonings. Place the duck liver in a bowl, remove the veins, season and moisten with the armagnac and port. Press the whole liver into a terrine and cover with cling film. Leave to marinate for 12 hours in the refrigerator.

Place the terrine in a shallow pan filled with hot water, cover with aluminium foil and transfer to a slow oven (140°C/285°F, Gas Mark 2). Bake for around 50 minutes or until the thermometer indicates that the temperature at the centre of the terrine is 54°C/129°F. Remove the terrine, cover with a piece of cardboard and weight it heavily. Leave to cool at room temperature then set aside in the refrigerator.

The following day, melt the fat that has risen above the cardboard and pour it over the liver in the terrine. Leave several days in the refrigerator before serving.

Serve on warm toast lightly sprinkled with coarse sea salt and freshly milled pepper.

Duckling with braised turnips, p80

One 3lb (1.5kg) duckling

4oz (125g) small onions

2fl oz (50ml) white wine

9fl oz (250ml) chicken stock

2fl oz (50ml) Madeira

Oil, butter, sugar, salt, pepper

Brown the trussed and seasoned duckling in a casserole until nicely golden. Add the onions to the casserole, leave them to brown, then add the Madeira, white wine and chicken stock. Cover and simmer for 50 minutes, basting regularly with the cooking juices. Meanwhile place the peeled and cut turnips in a saucepan with sufficient water to cover. Add a knob of butter, two pinches of salt and one teaspoon of sugar. Cook until all the water has evaporated.

Five minutes before the duck has finished cooking, add the turnips to the casserole and leave to turn jammy in the meat juices.

Foie gras and truffle turnover, p34

1 sheet ready-rolled flaky pastry

6 small truffles

Good 5oz (160g) foie gras

1 beaten egg, salt, pepper

Using a pastry cutter, cut out circles of pastry four inches in diameter, and brush the edges with a little beaten egg. Place a thin slice of foie gras in the centre and top with a truffle. Seal the turnovers by folding over the edges and pressing them down with your fingers. Brush with beaten egg and cook in a moderate oven for 20 minutes (170°C/340°F, Gas Mark 6).

Grilled rib of beef with pepper sauce and pommes paillasson, p88

2 ribs of beef

Oil, salt, pepper

FOR THE SAUCE:

Flat tsp (10g) peppercorns (five-pepper blend)

2fl oz (50ml) cognac, 1 glass dry white wine

7fl oz (200ml) meat stock

Salt

Brush each rib of beef on both sides with oil and set aside at room temperature for at least 20 minutes before grilling.

To make the pepper sauce: Sweat the chopped shallots in butter over a low heat then add the coarsely ground peppercorns. Flambé with the cognac, de-glaze with the white wine and cook until completely

Quantities for six people

155

reduced. Add the meat juices and cook over a very low heat for 10 minutes. Adjust the seasonings and thicken the sauce with a few knobs of fresh butter.

Serve the steaks with thin, crispy grated potato cakes and a garnish of pepper sauce.

Grilled spare ribs with roasted figs, p104

3lb (1.2kg) pork spare ribs

12 figs

1oz (25g) butter, 3-4fl oz (100ml) olive oil

Rosemary, thyme, summer savory

Coriander seeds, sugar, salt, pepper

Split the spare ribs into six equal portions. Plunge into a saucepan of cold water, bring to the boil and cook for five minutes, adding salt. Then drain and dry the ribs very carefully and place them in a dish, sprinkling with the herbs and olive oil. Cover with cling film and leave to marinate for two hours. Finish the ribs by barbecuing over hot coals. (Pre-cooking as in this recipe gives the meat a softer texture once barbecued.)

Make a cut in each fig, dot it with a knob of butter, sprinkle with sugar and roast in a hot oven (180°C/355°F, Gas Mark 7) for 10-12 minutes.

Grilled turbot with fennel, p62

6 turbot escalopes, each about 7oz (180g)

4 fennel bulbs, few sprigs lemon thyme

3 tbsp olive oil, juice 1 lemon

Sugar, salt, freshly milled pepper

Lightly brush the fish with olive oil and sprinkle with leaves of lemon thyme. Place in a dish covered with cling film and set aside in the refrigerator for 30 minutes.

Meanwhile heat the remaining olive oil in a heavy-based pan, then add the shredded fennel together with a pinch of sugar and salt. Cover and simmer over a low heat for 35-40 minutes (adding water if necessary). When the fennel is cooked, grill the turbot escalopes on both sides then arrange them on a bed of stewed fennel. Serve garnished with fennel fronds.

Ham with Epoisses cheese sauce, p102

6 thick slices ham off the bone

8fl oz (200ml) broth (ham cooking juices)

1 Epoisses cheese

8fl oz (200ml) cream

Salt, pepper

Heat the ham until warm in a little of the stock. Scrape the rind off the Epoisse cheese. In a separate saucepan, reduce the rest of the stock with the cream, then add the cheese a little at a time, beating well to obtain a smooth, creamy consistency. Adjust the seasoning to taste.

Serve the ham coated with the sauce.

Jugged boar with chestnut purée, p114

The recipe is the same as for jugged hind, using shoulder or neck meat, and replacing the mushrooms with chestnut purée. Note that haunch of boar is generally reserved for roasting.

Jugged hind with mushrooms, p112

Good 3lb (1.3kg) assorted cuts of hind (shoulder, breast, neck)

1 carrot (coarse-diced), 1 onion (coarse-diced)

1 tbsp flour

5fl oz (150ml) pig's blood

1 shallot, 2 cloves garlic

1pt 15fl oz (1 litre) good red wine

2fl oz (50ml) vinegar, cognac

1 tbsp (20ml) oil

1 bouquet garni (thyme, bay leaf, celery, parsley stalks)

Place the meat pieces and vegetables in a dish with the red wine, a trickle of oil and a dash of cognac. Leave to marinate for 24 hours in the refrigerator. On the day, strain the meat and brown it in a casserole with a little oil. Add the vegetables and cook until jammy. Meanwhile bring the marinade to the boil and when it starts to bubble, skim and strain through a fine sieve. Sprinkle the meat and vegetables with one tablespoon of flour, stir well, then add the strained marinade, the bouquet garni and two glasses of water. Cover and simmer over a very low heat for two hours.

Remove the meat from the cooking liquid, drain well and set aside. Strain the cooking juices and beat in the blood, being careful not to let the sauce boil. Adjust the seasonings, return the meat to the sauce and simmer for 15 minutes (still taking care

not to let it boil). Just before serving, add some sautéed wild mushrooms (Chanterelles, wild Black Trumpet Chanterelles).

Lampreys Bordeaux-style with slow-cooked leeks, p68

2lb 4oz (1kg) lamprey eel

8-10 leeks

20fl oz (500ml) red wine

5oz (150g) diced ham

1oz (25g) butter, 2 tbsp flour

4fl oz (100ml) cognac

1 onion, bouquet garni, salt, pepper

Suspend the eel from some form of hook, head upwards. Pour a glass of red wine into a large bowl, then cut the tail off the eel and collect the blood in the same bowl.

Scald the fish for a few minutes then scrape the skin with a knife to remove any slime. Chop the eel into chunks, removing the cartilage that runs down the back, and place the pieces in a deep bowl. Cover with the wine and blood, season with salt and pepper and add the onion rings.

Peel the leeks, retaining only the white, then soften them in a saucepan with a little oil. Add the diced ham, sprinkle with the flour and moisten with red wine. Add the bouquet garni, salt and pepper and cook over a low heat until reduced by three-quarters.

Add the eel chunks (saving the blood marinade) and continue cooking over a low heat for 45 minutes. Remove the bouquet garni, then thicken the sauce with the blood marinade. Serve with croutons.

Langres cheese vol-au-vents, p134

1 Langres cheese

6 crispy, freshly baked vol-au-vent shells

De-rind the cheese and warm in a hot oven for five minutes. Split the puff pastry shells into two. Fill one half with a spoonful of the creamy warmed cheese and cover with the other half. Serve immediately.

Lemon meringue pie, p144

1 pre-cooked shortbread pastry base

8fl oz (200ml) lemon juice

Grated rind of two lemons

10oz (300g) sugar

7 eggs

Quantities for six people

7-8oz (220g) butter

Meringue made with 2 large egg whites and 4oz (100-125g) caster sugar

To prepare the lemon filling: Beat together the sugar and the eggs, then add the grated lemon rind. Heat the lemon juice then add the eggs one at a time. Cook over a low heat, stirring constantly for 5-6 minutes. Pour the lemon mixture into a large bowl and beat in the butter a knob at a time, stirring thoroughly. Now pour this filling into the pastry base and leave to set in the refrigerator for at least six hours. A few minutes before serving, garnish the tart with a generous amount of meringue. Place under a hot grill for two minutes until the meringue turns a lovely golden brown and serve immediately.

Mixed leaves with roasted goat's cheese, p128

6 Crottins de Chavignol (small goat's cheeses)

6 slices bread, half lemon

Assortment ready-prepared young leaves (lambs' lettuce, oak leaf lettuce, purslane, radicchio, roquette)

2fl oz (50ml) chicken stock

2fl oz (50ml) peanut oil

Mixed herbs (chives, chervil, flat-leafed parsley)

Mix the lemon juice with a pinch of salt and pepper then combine with the oil and chicken stock, beating well. Cut the goat's cheeses in half width-wise and place them on the bread slices. Grill in a hot oven for eight minutes (180°C/355°F, Gas Mark 7). Toss the lettuces in the sauce. Arrange a bed of lettuce on each plate, top with the goat's cheese and sprinkle with the chopped herbs. Serve warm.

Mouclade (mussels in a cream sauce), p40

3pt 10fl oz (2 litres) mussels

3oz (80g) butter, 3oz (80g) flour, salt, pepper

1 clove garlic, 1 egg yolk, half lemon

Chopped parsley, curry powder

Cook the mussels in a saucepan over a low heat until they open. Remove one half of each shell then set the mussels aside in a warm place.

Prepare a roux with the butter and flour. Moisten with half a pint (quarter litre) of the mussel cooking juices, adding salt and pepper and a pinch of crushed garlic. Set on the heat to cook, stirring in the egg yoke and lemon juice to thicken. Flavour with a pinch of curry and sprinkle with chopped parsley. Arrange the mussels on a dish and coat with the sauce before serving.

Oursinade (sea urchins), p42

To open a sea urchin, turn it upside down and, using the point of a knife, remove the mouth then cut off this flat side with a pair of scissors and discard it together with any liquid. What remains is the star-shaped body cavity containing the orangey tongues – the only edible part of a sea urchin. Either scoop this out with a teaspoon and eat it directly, or pound it to a paste and use it to stuff eggs or as flavour for a butter sauce or mayonnaise.

Pan-fried calf's liver with raspberry vinegar and blackcurrants, p98

6 slices calf's liver

Dash oil, 1oz (25g) butter, 1 tbsp flour

2fl oz (50ml) meat stock

2 tbsp blackcurrant berries

Raspberry vinegar, salt, pepper

Lightly dredge the liver slices in flour, season and sauté in a frying pan. Remove and set aside on warm serving plates. De-glaze the pan with raspberry vinegar, then reduce the juices, adding the meat stock and blackcurrant berries. Pour this sauce over the liver slices and serve immediately.

Parsley ham, p20

1 lightly salted cooked ham (1lb/500g)

1 veal knuckle, 2 veal trotters, 6 shallots

1 glass white Burgundy wine, 1 tbsp vinegar

1 bunch chervil, tarragon, parsley

2oz (50g) chopped parsley

Pinch thyme, 1 bay leaf, salt, pepper

De-salt the ham overnight. The next day, place it in a casserole with the veal knuckle and trotters, the herbs, the shallots and the white wine. Cover with water and simmer for two hours. Then remove the meats and chop them into large cubes, mixing up fat and lean. Set aside in a mixing bowl. Clarify the cooking liquid so as to obtain a richly coloured jelly. As soon as it starts to thicken, add the chopped parsley and vinegar and pour it over the ham. Leave to cool and serve straight from the bowl.

Pear and Roquefort tart, p138

1 sheet ready-rolled flaky pastry dough

3 very ripe pears

4oz (100g) Roquefort cheese, 1 tbsp sugar

Cut the pastry dough into six inch (15cm) wide strips. Peel, halve and shred the pears, and spread on the pastry strips. Sprinkle with sugar and bake at 180°C/355°F, Gas Mark 7, for 20-25 minutes. Straight out of the oven, dot them with equal amounts of Roquefort cheese and serve immediately while the cheese is still melting.

Pigeon with cabbage, p84

6 small pigeons

1oz (25g) butter

2oz (50g) lardons

Half a blanched green cabbage

9fl oz (250ml) chicken stock

1 glass dry white wine

1 onion, 1 clove garlic

Thyme, bay leaf, salt, pepper

Brown the pigeons in butter in a casserole then remove and set aside. In the same pan, sauté the lardons, the chopped onion and crushed garlic.

Line the bottom of the casserole with the blanched cabbage leaves, place the pigeons on top and moisten with the white wine and chicken stock. Add the thyme, the bay leaf, salt and pepper. Cover and simmer for about 15 minutes over a very low heat. Remove the pigeons and keep warm. Continue cooking the cabbage for 20-25 minutes (adding more water if necessary but don't overdo the liquid – there should be very little juice in the pan).

Serve the pigeons on a bed of well-stewed cabbage.

Pikeperch with star anise and bamboo shoots, p54

6 pikeperch steaks

4fl oz (100ml) dry white wine

8fl oz (200ml) fish stock

8fl oz (200ml) single cream

4oz (100g) bamboo shoots

Quantities for six people

157

1oz (25g) butter

1shallot, 2 star anise, salt, pepper

Sprinkle a layer of chopped shallots into an ovenproof dish and place the fish steaks on top. Season with salt and pepper and moisten with three tablespoons of fish stock. Cover with aluminium foil.

To prepare the sauce: Combine the remaining fish stock with the white wine and reduce by half. Add the cream and the star anise and leave to infuse for 10 minutes. Then remove the star anise and blend the sauce in a mixer.

Put the dish of fish (still covered with foil) in a hot oven and bake for 15 minutes (180°C/355°F, Gas Mark 7). Meanwhile, fry the bamboo shoots in a knob of butter.

Remove the fish from the oven, drain them well and serve in soup plates, each on a bed of bamboo shoots and coated with the star-anise sauce.

Plain chocolate fondant, p148

6oz (180g) plain chocolate

7oz (200g) butter, 7 eggs

7oz (200g) sugar, 1-2oz (40g) flour

The previous day, break the chocolate up into small pieces and melt together with the butter in a bowl. Beat the eggs, sugar and flour until smooth and creamy, then combine with the melted butter and chocolate, mixing well. Pour into small buttered ramekins and chill in the freezer overnight.

On the day, transfer the ramekins to a hot oven (180°C/355°F, Gas Mark 7) and cook for 7-10 minutes depending on the consistency desired.

Turn the fondants out onto a dish. You should be able to see the soft, runny interior through the crisp exterior.

Poached eggs en meurette, p26

8 eggs, 8fl oz (200ml) wine vinegar

FOR THE SAUCE:

1 chopped shallot

4oz (100g) mushrooms

2oz (100g) butter

10-12fl oz (300ml) red wine

1 tbsp chopped chives

4oz (100g) lardons

4 slices bread

1 clove garlic, 1 stock cube

Salt, freshly milled pepper

Mix the vinegar with 3-4 pints (two litres) water and bring to simmering point. Break the eggs one at a time into a cup then slide them one by one into the simmering water. Poach the eggs for four minutes, then drain and set aside.

To make the sauce: Heat a knob of butter in a frying pan and sauté the shallot together with the cleaned and sliced mushrooms and the lardons. Moisten with the red wine and flambé when the sauce starts to boil. Add a stock cube, reduce for 10 minutes then add the butter, a knob at a time, whisking vigorously. Season this sauce with salt and pepper and strain it through a fine sieve. Serve the eggs coated with sauce, on slices of toast rubbed with garlic.

Potted duck with lentils, p82

6 potted duck thighs

1lb 2oz (500g) green lentils (preferably French du Puy)

1 onion, chopped, 1 carrot, peeled and chopped

1 bacon rasher, diced

Thyme, pepper

Garlic and parsley for the 'persillade' (optional)

Fry the onion, carrot and bacon in a little of the duck fat until golden. Add the lentils, the thyme, half a glass of water and simmer for 15 minutes.

Place the duck pieces in an ovenproof dish and brown in a hot oven (180°C/355°F, Gas Mark 7) for 10 minutes. Pour off the fat and mix the lentils with the duck.

Serve immediately, sprinkled if you wish with persillade (chopped parsley and garlic).

Quail with grapes, p74

6 quail

6 rashers larding bacon

11oz (300g) plump red grapes

2 tbsp unripe grape juice (verjus)

3-4 fl oz (100ml) chicken stock

1 tbsp oil, 1oz (25g) butter

1 small onion

Salt, pepper

Bard each quail with a bacon rasher then brown the birds in a casserole with a knob of butter and a drizzle of oil for 10-15 minutes.

Add the finely chopped onion. De-glaze the casserole with the grape juice, add the chicken stock, cover and cook for 15-20 minutes. Add the grapes roughly three minutes before the cooking time is up.

Red mullet with tapenade, p66

6 small red mullet, scaled but not gutted

2 tbsp olive oil, 1oz (25g) butter

4oz (100g) black tapenade

14oz (400g) long-grain French rice (Camargue)

2oz (50g) lightly salted bacon

2 small new onions

Sprig rosemary, salt, pepper

To prepare the rice: Sauté the onions and bacon in a tablespoon of the olive oil. Add the rice together with one pint (600ml) of hot water, a pinch of salt and a few needles of rosemary. Cover and cook over a very low heat for 18 minutes (the rice will absorb all the liquid during cooking).

Lightly dredge the red mullet in flour and fry until golden in a hot frying pan with the rest of the olive oil and butter. Remove the fish (saving the cooking juices) and serve each one garnished on the plate with a scoop of tapenade, a spoonful of rice and a ribbon of the buttery cooking juices.

Roast Camembert with apples, p132

1 Camembert

3 apples

1oz (25g) butter

6 slices farmhouse bread

Quarter the apples then brown for three minutes a side in hot butter. De-rind the Camembert and warm in a hot oven (180°C/355°F, Gas Mark 7) for five minutes. Divide the sautéed apple quarters between the bread slices and top with a generous spoonful of creamy cheese.

Roast goose Sarlat-style, p86

1 trussed oven-ready goose

1oz (25g) goose fat

7oz (200g) fresh ceps, 2 Périgord truffles

3lb (1.2kg) potatoes

Salt, pepper

Place the seasoned goose in a roasting pan with three glasses of water and roast in a hot oven (170°C/340°F, Gas Mark 6) for one

Quantities for six people

and a half hours, basting regularly.

Meanwhile peel and thickly slice the potatoes then fry them in the goose fat. Season with salt and pepper. Sauté the ceps separately then add them to the potatoes along with the slivers of truffles.

When the goose is cooked, drain off excess fat and surround it with the potatoes. Then return the dish to a slow oven and bake for 10 minutes so as to obtain a good blend of flavours.

Roast kid with chestnuts, p110

Half a whole kid
2lb 15oz (800g) peeled chestnuts
5 tomatoes
2fl oz (50ml) olive oil
2 heads of garlic
Thyme, wild thyme, rosemary, savory
Salt, pepper

Brush the kid with oil, sprinkle with the herbs and place in a roasting pan. Add the halved heads of garlic and the tomatoes. Season generously with salt and pepper. Place in a hot oven (180°C/355°F, Gas Mark 7) and roast for 30-40 minutes per pound, basting regularly with the cooking juices. If the meat browns too quickly, cover with aluminium foil. Shortly before the cooking time is up, add the peeled chestnuts and bake until jammy in the meat juices.

Roasted lobster with mild spices, p44

1 lobster
1oz (25g) butter, 1 tbsp olive oil, 2 shallots
1 glass Palette white wine
5fl oz (150ml) fresh cream
Pinch paprika and allspice
Mixed herbs, salt, pepper

Slice the lobster tail into medallion-sized pieces, setting aside the coral. Make a lobster shell stock with the leftover carcass. Take a heavy-based saucepan and sear the lobster medallions in a drizzle of hot oil and butter. When the shell turns bright red, sprinkle with paprika and allspice, add the chopped shallots and moisten with the white wine. (Beware of over-doing the liquid, or the texture of the meat will become too soft.) Season with salt and pepper, then cover and cook over a very low heat for 20

minutes. Next, remove the lobster while you make the sauce. Start by de-glazing the pan with the lobster shell stock then thicken the juices with the coral and the cream. Place the lobster medallions in the sauce, adding a pinch of chopped mixed herbs to taste.

Salmis of guinea fowl with white kidney beans, p72

1 boned guinea fowl with giblets
4oz (100g) finely minced sausage meat
1lb 5oz (600g) cooked white kidney beans
1 onion, 2 cloves garlic
8fl oz (200ml) meat stock
1oz (25g) butter, 2fl oz (50ml) oil
Parsley, chives, tarragon, salt, pepper

Make a stuffing by combining the sausage meat with the giblets and the chopped herbs. Add seasoning and a touch of garlic to flavour.

Use this mixture to stuff the guinea fowl, then tie the bird into a roast with string and place in an ovenproof dish. Drizzle with oil, add the chopped onion and roast in a hot oven for 20 minutes (180°C/355°F, Gas Mark 7). Remove the dish from the oven, add the drained beans, moisten with a little stock then return to the oven for a further 20 minutes. Baste sparingly but frequently, bearing in mind that this is not a highly sauced dish.

Serve the bird sliced, on a bed of kidney beans.

Salmon with sorrel, p58

6 x 4oz (120g) salmon steaks
1 glass dry white wine, 1 glass fish stock
2 tbsp dry white vermouth
2 shallots
8fl oz (200ml) single cream
3-4oz (80g) fresh sorrel leaves
Coarse sea salt, pepper

Season the salmon steaks with salt and pepper, then place them skin-side down in an oiled, non-stick frying pan. Cook over a very low heat for 8-10 minutes.

To prepare the sauce: Pour the white wine, the fish stock and the vermouth into a saucepan. Add the chopped shallots then reduce the liquid by half. Combine with the single cream then reduce again until the sauce is thick and creamy. Sprinkle with the

chopped sorrel leaves and adjust the seasoning. Spoon the sauce onto warmed serving plates, top with a salmon steak and sprinkle with coarse sea salt.

Scallops with white butter sauce, p48

18 scallops
Few drops oil, salt, pepper
FOR THE SAUCE:
3 shallots
4fl oz (100ml) white wine
Dash white wine vinegar
5oz (150g) semi-salted butter

Cut the scallops in half, width-wise. Heat a drop of oil in a non-stick frying pan until good and hot, then sauté the scallops for about two minutes a side. Remove them when golden on the outside but still pearly white inside. Set aside just long enough to make the sauce as follows:

Dice the butter and place in the refrigerator. Boil together the white wine and shallots until completely reduced. Then combine with the butter over a low heat, adding a knob at a time and whisking continuously. Finish off with a dash of vinegar, salt and pepper. Serve the scallops immediately on a bed of creamy sauce.

Note that it's always preferable to make the sauce at the last minute since it does have a tendency to collapse if made in advance.

Seafood lasagne, p124

7oz (200g) fresh lasagne
6lb 12oz (3kg) shellfish (cockles, mussels, clams)
4oz (100g) peeled shrimps
1 clove garlic, 1 tbsp chopped parsley
1oz (25g) breadcrumbs
9fl oz (250ml) fish stock
8fl oz (200ml) single cream
1 glass dry white wine, salt, pepper

Cook the shellfish à la marinière (in a shallot and white-wine broth) then remove them from their shells, saving any juice.

Reduce the broth with the shellfish juices and the cream. When the liquid starts to thicken, add the shellfish, the shrimps, the crushed garlic and parsley. Season with salt and pepper.

Spread a layer of this mixture over the bottom of an ovenproof dish, and cover with

Quantities for six people

a layer of lasagne. Add another layer of the shellfish filling, then a final layer of lasagne. Top with a coating of sauce and sprinkle with breadcrumbs. Brown in a hot oven for 15 minutes (180°C/355°F, Gas Mark 7).

Seven-hour leg of lamb with broad beans, p106

5lb (2.5kg) leg of lamb

10 cloves garlic, 3 large onions, 4 tomatoes

2 glasses white wine

7fl oz (200ml) meat stock

1lb 12oz (800g) pre-boiled broad beans

2fl oz (50ml) oil, 1oz (25g) butter

Thyme, bay leaf, rosemary, salt, pepper

Brown the lamb in a large casserole with the oil and butter. Pour off some of the excess fat, add the coarsely chopped onions, quartered tomatoes, crushed garlic and bouquet garni.

Cook over a low heat for a few minutes, stirring constantly. Add the white wine and the meat stock. Cover and bake in a slow oven (140°C/285°F, Gas Mark 2) for seven hours (adding a little water if necessary during cooking).

Carefully remove the lamb from the oven and keep it warm. Strain the sauce, adjust the seasoning and pour it over the lamb. Serve the meat on a bed of fresh, buttered broad beans.

Snails with garlic and herbs, p28

6 doz canned snails plus empty snail shells

FOR THE GARLIC BUTTER:

11oz (300g) butter

1oz (20g) ground almonds

3 cloves garlic, 2 shallots, 1 bunch parsley

1 pinch salt and pepper

A few drops Pastis

Drain the snails thoroughly and place them inside the shells.

Cream together the butter, shallots and an equal quantity of chopped parsley. Add the ground almonds, crushed garlic, salt and pepper, together with a few drops of Pastis (optional).

Fill the snail shells with the garlic butter, place them in a suitable (oven-proof) dish and bake in a very hot oven for five minutes (190°C/375°F, Gas Mark 9).

Stuffed cabbage with mild spices, p120

1 green cabbage

9oz (250g) of round-grain rice

1 onion, 1 clove garlic

4fl oz (100ml) oil

4fl oz (100ml) meat stock

1 tbsp (5g) paprika, 1 tbsp (5g) cinnamon

Salt, pepper

Blanch the cabbage leaves in boiling salted water. Fry the onion and crushed garlic in the oil. Add the rice and stir until all the grains are translucent. Add the spices, season with salt and pepper, and moisten with two glasses of water. Cook on a very low heat for 10 minutes, stirring continuously and adding extra water if necessary.

Line a casserole with the blanched cabbage leaves (saving a few large leaves for the top layer), cover with a thin layer of rice then a layer of leaves and repeat until all the rice and cabbage has been used up. Cover with the leaves previously set aside. Add the stock and another glass of water. Cover and bake for 30 minutes (170-180°C/340-355°F, Gas Mark 6-7). Serve directly from the casserole.

Tagliatelle Bolognese, p126

9oz (250g) fresh tagliatelle

1 can chopped tomatoes

7oz (200g) minced beef

1 onion, 2 cloves garlic

4fl oz (200ml) olive oil

Thyme, rosemary, oregano, salt, pepper

Brown the chopped onion and meat in hot olive oil in a frying pan. Add the garlic and the tomatoes, seasoning and herbs. Cover and simmer over a very low heat for 30-40 minutes.

Cook the tagliatelle 'al dente' in a large quantity of boiling salted water. Drain and place a portion on each plate. Top with a generous amount of Bolognese sauce and sprinkle with grated Parmesan. Serve immediately.

Tapenade-stuffed saddle of lamb with roasted cherry tomatoes, p108

1 whole saddle of lamb, boned

4oz (125g) black olive tapenade

2 tbsp olive oil, 1oz butter

10 small, very ripe fresh tomatoes

4fl oz (120ml) meat stock

Fresh thyme leaves, salt, pepper

Open the lamb flat, coat the inside with the tapenade and sprinkle with thyme. Roll and tie the meat to form a roast. Place in an ovenproof dish with olive oil and butter and cook in a pre-heated oven (180°C/ 355°F, Gas Mark 7), allowing 12 minutes per pound. When the meat starts to brown, turn it over and baste generously with the cooking juices.

Five minutes before the cooking time is up, arrange the tomatoes around the lamb. Make the gravy once the lamb is cooked: Remove the meat and tomatoes from the pan, pour off excess fat and add a glass of water. Bring to the boil and check seasoning. Serve the meat with the oven-dried tomatoes and the gravy.

Trout with almonds, p56

6 gutted trout, each about 10oz (250g)

4oz (100g) butter, 1 tbsp flour

3oz (75g) flaked almonds, juice 1 lemon

Salt, pepper

Dry the trout thoroughly and dredge in flour. Heat a tablespoon of butter in a large frying pan, add the trout and brown on both sides. Lower the heat and continue cooking for 10-12 minutes, basting continuously with the butter. Remove the trout from the pan, strain off the fat and arrange them in a serving dish, drizzling with the lemon juice. Fry the almonds in a separate frying pan with the remaining butter and sprinkle them over the trout.

Veal escalope with citrus fruits and chicory, p94

6 veal escalopes (cut from the tenderloin)

1oz (25g) butter, dash oil

6 cooked chicory, 3 tangerines

1 glass white beer

3-4fl oz (100ml) single cream

Sugar, salt, pepper

Cut the chicory in half then braise them in a frying pan with a knob of butter and a pinch of sugar and cook until caramelised. Set aside on a plate.

Heat a knob of butter in a frying pan, brown the veal escalopes and set aside. De-glaze

Quantities for six people

the pan with the beer and reduce the juices by three-quarters. Add the cream and adjust the seasoning. Peel and quarter the tangerines, removing all the pith, and toss them in the nut-brown butter until just warm. Place the escalopes on individual plates, each on a bed of braised chicory, garnished with the tangerine quarters, topped with sauce and dotted with julienne strips of tangerine peel (optional).

Venison grand veneur with celery chips, p116

2lb (900g) venison fillets or 12 venison cutlets

1 pinch thyme leaves

1 tbsp (5g) juniper berries

1 tbsp (5g) peppercorns

1 tbsp (5g) coriander seeds

1 bay leaf

1 dash wine vinegar, 1 dash armagnac

Olive oil, salt

FOR THE GRAND VENEUR SAUCE:

9fl oz (250ml) sauce poivrade (made with reduced game stock – or failing that, strong meat stock)

1 tbsp redcurrant jelly

2fl oz (50ml) fresh cream

Salt, pepper

FOR THE CELERY CHIPS:

1 celeriac

1 tbsp flour, oil for frying

The day before, place the venison fillet in a casserole with the ground spices, vinegar, dash of armagnac and oil. Cover with cling film and marinate overnight (there should be just enough marinade to coat the meat).

On the day, heat some oil and butter in a frying pan and sauté the venison fillet until cooked. Remove the meat from the pan and leave it to relax for a few minutes before slicing (keeping it warm).

To make the grand veneur sauce: Heat the sauce poivrade, add the redcurrant jelly and the fresh cream. Adjust the seasonings and pour the sauce into a gravy boat. Some people like to add a few fresh blackcurrants before serving.

To make the celery chips: Quarter the celeriac and round off the corners. Slice each piece thinly into slices approximately one-eighth of an inch thick, then dredge in flour, shaking off the excess. Deep-fry until golden, drain on kitchen paper and sprinkle lightly with salt.

Warm asparagus in gribiche sauce, p24

24 asparagus

Rock salt

FOR THE SAUCE:

1 hard-boiled egg, 1 tsp mustard

7fl oz (200ml) oil

2 tbsp capers, 1 chopped shallot

2 tbsp chopped herbs (chervil, tarragon, chives)

White vinegar, salt, pepper

Peel the asparagus and cook in a generous quantity of boiling salted water. Drain on a tea towel.

To make the sauce: Mix the hard-boiled egg yolk with the mustard and beat in the oil drop by drop. Add the chopped hard-boiled egg white, the capers, herbs and shallot. Season with salt and pepper and thin the sauce with a dash of white vinegar.

Warm salt cod brandade, p50

1lb 5oz (600g) fillets of salted cod

1 potato

4fl oz (100ml) milk

10fl oz (300ml) olive oil

1 clove of garlic, 1 lemon

Pepper

Soak the cod for 12 hours, changing the water several times. Remove the skin and bones. Place the cod in a casserole, cover with cold water and cook over a very low heat for 15 minutes. Drain the fish then, using a pestle and mortar, pound the flesh to a fine paste. Combine with the cooked potato and crushed clove of garlic. Warm the oil and milk then drizzle them in slowly, working them continuously into the potato and fish mixture. Add a few drops of lemon juice and white pepper.

Serve the brandade warm with a garnish of fried croutons.

White fish terrine with aioli sauce, p14

4 fillets scorpion fish, 4 fillets sole

4 fillets red mullet

18fl oz fish stock, 2fl oz dry white wine

2oz courgettes, I red pepper, 1 leek

6 leaves gelatine

Pinch saffron, salt, pepper

Dice the vegetables and cook in water for five minutes. Heat the fish stock, adding a pinch of salt, the white wine and the saffron. Plunge in the fish fillets, cook for five minutes then strain.

Mix the softened gelatine leaves with 11fl oz (300ml) of the fish stock and leave to cool. Line a terrine dish with greaseproof paper, then fill with a layer of the fish fillets, followed by a coating of the gelatine mixture, then a tablespoon of diced vegetables. Chill for five minutes, then repeat the layering process until all the ingredients have been used up. Leave to set in the refrigerator for 12 hours.

Aioli

1 small cooked potato, 6 garlic cloves

6fl oz olive oil

1 egg yoke, 1 lemon

Salt

Using a pestle and mortar, reduce the garlic to a smooth paste, mash with the potato and season with a pinch of salt. Combine with the egg yoke, then slowly stir in the olive oil, a drop at a time, until the sauce is good and thick and all the oil has been incorporated. Season with the lemon juice.

Yellow plum tart, p142

1 sheet ready-rolled shortbread pastry dough

1lb 12oz (800g) small yellow plums

2oz (50g) confectioner's custard

Line a greased flan case with the pastry. Spread with a thin layer of confectioner's custard then fill with the pitted plums. Dust with sugar and bake in a hot oven for 30-35 minutes (180°C/355°F, Gas Mark 7).

Quantities for six people

AJACCIO ROUGE

Clos d'Alzeto
20151 Sari d'Orcino
04 95 52 24 67

Clos Capitoro
20166 Porticcio
04 95 25 19 61

Domaine Comte Peraldi
20167 Mezzavia
04 95 22 37 30

ALSACE GEWURZTRAMINER
VENDANGES TARDIVES

Cave de la Pfaffenheim
68250 Pfaffenheim
03 89 78 08 08

Domaine Blanck et Fils
68240 Kientzheim
03 89 78 23 56

Domaine Seppi Landemann
68570 Soultzmatt
03 89 47 09 33

ALSACE PINOT NOIR ROUGE

Domaine du Clos Saint-Landelain
68250 Rouffach
03 89 78 58 00

Domaine Marcel Deiss
68750 Bergheim
03 89 73 63 37

Maison Hugel
68340 Riquewihr
03 89 47 92 15

ALSACE RIESLING

Domaine Ostertag
67680 Epfig
03 88 85 51 34

Domaine Schueller
68420 Husseren-les-Châteaux
03 89 49 31 54

Maison Léon Beyer
68420 Eguisheim
03 89 41 41 05

ALSACE RIESLING
VENDANGES TARDIVES

Domaine du Weinbach-Faller
68240 Kaysersberg
03 89 47 13 21

Domaine Zind Humbrecht
68230 Turckheim
03 89 27 02 05

Maison Trimbach
68150 Ribeauvillé
03 89 73 60 30

ALSACE TOKAY-PINOT GRIS

Domaine Rolly Gassmann
68590 Rorschwihr
03 89 73 33 06

Domaine Marc Tempe
68340 Zellenberg
03 89 47 85 22

Domaine Ernest Burn
68420 Gueberschwihr
03 89 49 20 68

ANJOU-VILLAGES BRISSAC

Château de Mongueret
49560 Nueil-sur-Layon
02 41 59 59 19

Domaine de Montgilet
49610 Juigné-sur-Loire
02 41 91 90 48

Domaine des Bonnes Gagnes
49320 Saint-Saturnin-sur-Loire
02 41 91 22 76

Domaine des Charbotières
49320 Saint-Jean-des-Mauvrets
02 41 91 22 87

Domaine des Rochelles
49320 Saint-Jean-des-Mauvrets
02 41 91 92 07

ARBOIS ROUGE

Domaine de la Pinte
39600 Arbois
03 84 66 60 47

Domaine Overnoy
39600 Pupillin
03 84 66 14 60

Domaine Rolet Père et Fils
39600 Arbois
03 84 66 00 05

Domaine André et Mireille Tissot
39600 Montigny-lès-Arsures
03 84 66 08 27

BANDOL ROUGE

Château de Pibarnon
83740 La Cadière-d'Azur
04 94 90 12 73

Château Pradeaux
83270 Saint-Cyr-sur-Mer
04 94 32 10 21

Château Vannières
83740 La Cadière-d'Azur
04 94 90 08 08

Domaine de Terrebrune
83190 Ollioules
04 94 74 01 30

Domaine Lafran-Veyrolles
83740 La Cadière-d'Azur
04 94 90 13 37

Domaine Tempiers
83330 Le Plan-du-Castelet
04 94 98 70 21

BANYULS

Cave l'Étoile
66650 Banyuls-sur-Mer
04 68 88 00 10

Domaine Mas Blanc
66650 Banyuls-sur-Mer
04 68 88 32 12

Domaine de la Rectorie
66650 Banyuls-sur-Mer
04 68 88 13 45

Domaine Vial-Magnères
66650 Banyuls-sur-Mer
04 68 88 31 04

BARSAC

Château Climens
33720 Barsac
05 56 27 15 33

Château Doisy Daëne
33720 Barsac
05 56 27 15 13

Château Nairac
33720 Barsac
05 56 27 16 16

BEAUJOLAIS ROUGE

Domaine des Terres Dorées
69380 Charnay
04 78 47 93 45

Domaine Dominique Piron
69910 Villié-Morgon
04 74 69 10 20

Domaine Jean-Charles Pivot
69430 Quincié-en-Beaujolais
04 74 04 30 32

Domaine Sante
71570 La Chapelle-de-Guinchay
03 85 33 82 81

Maison Duboeuf
71570 Romanèche-Thorins
03 85 35 34 20

BIÈRE BLANCHE

Brasseurs de Gayant
59502 Douai Cedex
03 27 93 26 22

Brasserie Heineken
92500 Rueil-Malmaison
01 47 14 36 50

Brasserie Interbrew France
59426 Armentières Cedex
03 20 48 30 30

Brasserie La Choulette
59111 Hordain Cedex
03 27 35 72 44

Brasserie Météor
67270 Hochfelden
03 88 02 22 22

Brasserie Pietra
20600 Furiani
04 95 30 14 70

Brasserie de Saint-Omer
62504 Saint-Omer Cedex
03 21 98 76 00

BONNEZEAUX

Château de Fesles
49380 Thouarcé
02 41 68 94 00

Domaine de Terrebrune
49380 Notre-Dame d'Allencon
02 41 54 01 99

Domaine des Gagneries
49380 Thouarcé
02 41 54 00 71

Domaine des Petits Quarts
49380 Faye-d'Anjou
02 41 54 03 00

Domaine René Renou
49380 Thouarcé
02 41 54 11 33

BORDEAUX CLAIRET

Château Bois Malot
33450 Saint-Loubès
05 56 38 94 18

Château Brethous
33360 Camblanes
05 56 20 77 76

Château Penin
33420 Genissac
05 57 24 46 98

BOURGUEIL ROUGE

Domaine Yannick Amirault
37140 Bourgueuil
02 47 97 78 07

Domaine Druet
37140 Benais
02 47 97 37 34

Domaine Gambier
37140 Ingrandes de Touraine
02 47 96 98 77

MaisonLame-Delille-Boucard
37140 Ingrandes-de-Touraine
02 47 96 98 54

CAHORS

Château du Cèdre
46700 Vire-sur-Lot
05 65 36 53 87

Château Goutoul
46700 Puy-l'Évêque
05 65 30 84 17

Château La Caminade
46140 Parnac
05 65 30 73 05

Châtau L agrezette
46140 Caillac
05 65 20 07 42

Clos Triguedina
46700 Puy-l'Évêque
05 65 21 30 81

CASSIS BLANC

Château de Fontcreuse
13260 Cassis
04 42 01 71 09

Clos Sainte-Magdeleine
13260 Cassis
04 42 01 70 28

Clos Val Bruyère
13830 Roquefort la Bedoule
04 42 73 14 60

Domaine du Bagnol
13260 Cassis
04 42 01 78 05

Domaine Saint-Louis
13260 Cassis
04 42 01 30 31

CHABLIS

Cave La Chablisienne
89800 Chablis
03 86 42 89 89

Domaine Dauvissat
89800 Chablis
03 86 42 11 58

Domaine Jean-Paul Droin
89800 Chablis
03 86 42 16 78

Domaine d'Élise
89800 Chablis
03 86 42 40 82

Domaine Laroche
89800 Chablis
03 86 42 89 00

Domaine Raveneau
89800 Chablis
03 86 42 17 46

Domaine William Fèvre
89800 Chablis
03 86 42 12 51

CHAMBOLLE-MUSIGNY

Château de Chambolle-Musigny
21220 Chambolle-Musigny
03 80 62 85 39

Domaine A.-F. Gros
21630 Pommard
03 80 22 61 85

Domaine Noellat
21220 Chambolle-Musigny
03 80 62 83 60

Domaine Robert Siruge
21700 Vosne-Romanée
03 80 61 00 64

Domaine Roumier
21220 Chambolle-Musigny
03 80 62 86 37

CHAMPAGNE
BLANC BRUT
Duval-Leroy
51130 Vertus
03 26 52 10 75

Gratien
51200 Épernay
03 26 54 38 20

Jacquesson et Fils
51530 Dizy
03 26 55 68 11

Lanson
51056 Reims Cedex
03 26 78 50 50

Laurent-Perrier
51150 Tours-sur-Marne
03 26 58 91 22

Moët et Chandon
51333 Épernay Cedex
03 26 51 20 00

Pol Roger
51200 Epernay
03 26 59 58 00

Pommery
51100 Reims
03 26 61 62 63

Roederer
51100 Reims
03 26 40 42 11

Ruinart
51100 Reims
03 26 77 51 51

Salon
51190 Le Mesnil-sur-Oger
03 26 57 51 65

Selosse
51190 Avize
03 26 57 53 56

Veuve Clicquot Ponsardin
51100 Reims
03 26 89 54 40

CHAMPAGNE ROSÉ
Billecart-Salmon
51160 Mareuil-sur-Ay
03 26 52 60 22

Bollinger
51160 Ay
03 26 53 33 66

Deutz
51160 Ay
03 26 55 15 11

Gosset
51160 Ay
03 26 55 14 18

Krug
51100 Reims
03 26 84 44 20

Taittinger
51061 Reims Cedex
03 26 85 45 35

Perrier-Jouët
51200 Épernay
03 26 53 38 00

CHÂTEAU-CHALON
Domaine Jean-Marie Courbet
39210 Nevy-sur-Seille
03 84 85 28 70

Domaine Jean Macle
39210 Château-Chalon
03 84 85 21 85

Domaine Jacques et Barbara
Durand-Perron
39210 Voiteur
03 84 44 66 80

CHÂTEAUNEUF-DU-PAPE BLANC
Château Mont-Redon
84230 Châteauneuf-du-Pape
04 90 83 72 75

Clos du Mont Olivet
84230 Châteauneuf-du-Pape
04 90 83 72 46

Domaine de Beaurenard
84230 Châteauneuf-du-Pape
04 90 83 71 79

Domaine de Nalys
84230 Châteauneuf-du-Pape
04 90 83 72 52

Domaine Marchand
84230 Châteauneuf-du-Pape
04 90 83 70 34

CHÂTEAUNEUF-DU-PAPE ROUGE
Château de Beaucastel
84360 Courthezon
04 90 70 41 00

Château de la Nerthe
84230 Châteauneuf-du-Pape
04 90 83 70 11

Château de Lagardine
84230 Châteauneuf-du-Pape
04 90 83 73 20

Château Rayas
84230 Châteauneuf-du-Pape
04 90 83 73 09

Clos des Papes
84230 Châteauneuf-du-Pape
04 90 83 70 13

Domaine du Vieux Télégraphe
84370 Bedarridès
04 90 33 00 31

Domaine de la Janasse
84350 Courthezon
04 90 70 86 29

Réserve des Célestins
84230 Châteauneuf-du-Pape
04 90 83 73 08

CIDRE
Le Père Jules
14100 Saint-Désir
02 31 61 14 57

Château de Hauteville
53250 Charchigne
02 43 03 95 72

Domaine Louis Dupont
14430 Victot-Pontfol
02 31 63 24 24

Les Vergers du Pays d'Auge
61120 Vimoutiers
02 33 36 28 21

Manoir La Brière des Fontaines
14340 Cambremer
02 31 63 01 09

Christian Drouin SA
42, rue du Général Giraud
76000 Rouen
02 35 89 99 54

CONDRIEU
Domaine Cuilleron
42410 Chavannay
04 74 87 02 37

Domaine Vernay
69420 Condrieu
04 74 59 52 22

Domaine Gaillard
42520 Malleval
04 74 87 13 10

Domaine Perret
42410 Chavannay
04 74 87 24 74

Domaine Villard
42410 Saint-Michel-sur-Rhône
04 74 56 87 76

CORTON-CHARLEMAGNE

Domainje Bonneau du Martray
21420 Pernand-Vergelesses
03 80 21 50 64

Domaine Chevalier
21550 Ladoix-Serrigny
03 80 26 46 30

Domaine du Pavillon
21200 Beaune
03 80 24 37 37

Domaine Michel Juillot
71640 Mercurey
03 85 98 99 89

COSTIÈRES DE NÎMES
ROUGE

Château Bolchet
30132 Caissargues
04 66 38 05 65

Château de Campuget
30129 Manduel
04 66 20 20 15

Châtau de l'Amarine
30129 Manduel
04 66 20 20 15

Château La Tuilerie
30900 Nîmes
04 66 70 07 52

Château Mas Neuf des Costières
30600 Gallican
04 66 73 33 23

Château Mourgues du Grès
30300 Beaucaire
04 66 59 46 10

CÔTE-RÔTIE

Domaine Jean-Michel Gerin
69420 Ampuis
04 74 56 16 56

Château d'Ampuis Guigal
69420 Ampuis
04 74 56 10 22

Domaine Burgaud
69420 Ampuis
04 74 56 11 86

Domaine Clusel Roch
69420 Ampuis
04 74 56 15 95

Domaine Duclaux
69420 Tupin-et-Semons
04 74 59 56 30

Domaine Jamet
69420 Ampuis
04 74 56 12 57

Domaine Stephan
69420 Tupin-et-Semons
04 75 56 62 66

COTEAUX DU LANGUEDOC BLANC

Château L'Hospitalet
11100 Narbonne
04 68 45 36 00

Château Puech-Haut
34160 Saint-Drezery
04 67 86 93 70

Domaine Les Aurelles
34720 Caux
04 67 98 46 21

Domaine Saint-Jean-de-Bebian
34120 Pézenas
04 67 98 13 60

COTEAUX DU LANGUEDOC ROUGE

Château de Capitoul
11100 Narbonne
04 68 49 23 30

Château de l'Engarran
34880 Laverune
04 67 47 00 02

Clos Marie
34270 Lauret
04 67 59 06 96

Domaine d'Aupilhac
34150 Montpeyroux
04 67 96 61 19

Domaine de l'Aiguelière
34150 Monpeyroux
04 67 96 61 78

Domaine Durand Camillo
34720 Caux
04 67 98 44 26

Domaine l'Hortus
34270 Valflaunes
04 67 55 31 20

Mas Bruguière
34270 Valflaunes
04 67 55 20 97

Mas Jullien
34725 Jonquières
04 67 96 60 04

CÔTES DE PROVENCE ROSÉ

Château Barbeyrolles
83580 Gassin
04 94 56 33 58

Château des Garcinières
83310 Cogolin
04 94 56 02 85

Château Les Valentines
83250 La Londe-les-Maures
04 94 15 95 50

Château Sainte-Roseline
83460 Les Arcs
04 94 99 50 30

Domaine de Saint-Ser
13114 Puyloubier
04 42 66 30 81

Mas de Cadenet
13530 Trets
04 42 29 21 59

CÔTES DU JURA
VIN DE PAILLE

Château d'Arlay
39140 Arlay
03 84 85 04 22

Domaine Badoz
39800 Poligny
03 84 37 11 85

Domaine Labet Père et Fils
39190 Rotalier
03 84 25 11 13

Domaine Rousselot Pailey
39210 Lavigny
03 84 25 38 38

FITOU

Château de Nouvelles
11480 La Palme
04 68 45 40 03

Domaine Les Mille Vignes
11480 La Palme
04 68 48 57 14

Domaine Bertrand Berge
11350 Paziols
04 68 45 41 73

Producteurs du Mont Tauch
11350 Tuchan
04 68 45 41 08

HERMITAGE BLANC

Cave de Tain
26600 Tain-l'Hermitage
04 75 08 20 87

Domaine Ferraton
26600 Tain-l'Hermitage
04 75 08 59 51

Domaine Marc Sorrel
26600 Tain-l'Hermitage
04 75 07 10 07

Domaine Jean-Louis Chave
07300 Mauves
04 75 08 24 63

Maison Paul Jaboulet Aîné
26600 La Roche-de-Glun
04 75 84 68 93

HERMITAGE ROUGE

Domaine Jean-Louis Chave
07300 Mauves
04 75 08 24 63

Domaine des Remizières
26600 Mercurol
04 75 07 44 28

Maison Chapoutier
26600 Tain-l'Hermitage
04 75 08 92 61

Maison Delas
07300 Saint-Jean-de-Muzols
04 75 08 60 30

Maison Paul Jaboulet Aîné
26600 La Roche-de-Glun
04 75 84 68 93

LES BAUX DE PROVENCE ROUGE

Château Romanin
13210 Saint-Rémy-de-Provence
04 90 92 45 87

Domaine Hauvette
13210 Saint-Rémy-de-Provence
04 90 92 03 90

Mas Sainte-Berthe
13520 Les Baux-de-Provence
04 90 54 39 01

L'ÉTOILE BLANC

Château de l'Étoile
39570 L'Étoile
03 84 47 33 07

Domaine Geneletti
39570 L'Étoile
03 84 47 46 25

Domaine de Montbourgeau
39570 L'Étoile
03 84 47 32 96

MÂCON BLANC

Domaine Bonhomme
71260 Viré
03 85 33 11 86

Domaine Guffens-Heynen
71960 Vergisson
03 85 35 84 22

Domaine Les Hauts d'Azenay
71260 Azé
04 74 50 90 60

Domaine Thévenet
71260 Clessé
03 85 36 94 03

Domaine Valette
71570 Chaintré
03 85 35 62 97

MADIRAN

Chapelle Lenclos
32400 Maumusson
05 62 69 78 11

Château Bouscassé
32400 Maumusson
05 62 69 74 67

Château d'Aydie
64330 Aydie
05 59 04 01 17

Château Laffitte-Teston
32400 Maumusson
05 62 69 74 58

Domaine Moureou
32400 Maumusson
05 62 69 78 11

MARGAUX ROUGE

Château Labégorce Zédé
33460 Margaux
05 57 88 71 31

Château Margaux
33460 Margaux
05 57 88 83 83

Château Rauzan-Segla
33460 Margaux
05 57 88 82 10

Château Monbrison
33460 Arsac
05 56 58 80 04

Château Palmer
33460 Margaux
05 57 88 72 72

Château Siran
33460 Lambarde
05 57 88 34 04

MEURSAULT BLANC

Domaine Jean-Marc Boillot
21630 Pommard
03 80 22 71 29

Domaine Coche Dury
21190 Meursault
03 80 21 24 12

Domaine des Comtes Lafon
21190 Meursault
03 80 21 22 17

Domaine Morey Pierre
21190 Meursault
03 80 21 21 03

Domaine Jacques Prieur
21190 Meursault
03 80 21 23 85

Domaine Roulot
21190 Meursalut
03 80 21 21 65

Maison Bouchard Père et Fils
21200 Beaune
03 80 24 80 24

MUSCADET DE SÈVRE-ET-MAINE

Château de la Preuille
85600 Saint-Hilaire-de-Loulay
02 51 46 32 32

Château La Ragotière
44330 Vallet-la-Regrippière
02 40 33 60 56

Domaine de l'Écu
44430 Le Landreau
02 40 06 40 91

Domaine de la Louvetrie
44690 La Haye-Fouassière
02 40 54 83 27

Domaine Luneau-Papin
44430 Le Landreau
02 40 06 45 27

MUSCAT DE MIREVAL

Domaine de la Capelle
34110 Mireval
04 67 78 15 14

Domaine du Moulinas
34110 Mireval
04 67 78 13 97

Domaine du Mas Neuf
34110 Vic-la-Gardiole
04 67 78 37 44

MUSCAT DU CAP CORSE

Clos Nicrosi
20247 Rogliano
04 95 35 41 17

Domaine Arena
20253 Patrimonio
04 95 37 08 27

Domaine Gentile
20217 Saint-Florent
04 95 37 01 54

Domaine Leccia
20232 Poggio d'Oletta
04 95 37 11 35

Domaine Pierretti
20228 Luri
04 95 35 01 03

NUITS-SAINT-GEORGES ROUGE

Clos de l'Arlot
21700 Prémeaux-Prissey
03 80 81 01 92

Domaine Prieuré Roch
21700 Nuits Saint-Georges
03 80 82 38 79

Maison Faiveley
21700 Nuits Saint-Georges
03 80 61 04 55

PACHERENC DU VIC-BILH

MOELLEUX
Château d'Aydie
64330 Aydie
05 59 04 01 17

Château Bouscassé
32400 Maumusson
05 62 69 74 67

Château Laffitte-Teston
32400 Maumusson
05 62 69 74 58

Producteurs de Plaimont
32400 Saint-Mont
05 62 69 62 87

PALETTE BLANC

Château Crémade
13100 Le Tholonet
04 42 68 92 66

Château Simone
13590 Meyreuil
04 42 66 92 58

PATRIMONIO BLANC

Domaine Arena
20253 Patrimonio
04 95 37 08 27

Domaine de Catarelli
20253 Patrimonio
04 95 37 02 84

Domaine Giudicelli
20213 Penta di Casinca
04 95 36 45 10

Domaine Leccia
20232 Poggio d'Oletta
04 95 37 11 35

PAUILLAC

Château La Bécasse
33250 Pauillac
05 56 59 07 14

Château La Tour
33250 Pauillac
05 56 73 19 80

Château Lafite Rothschild
33250 Pauillac
05 56 73 18 18

Château Lynch Bages
33250 Pauillac
05 56 73 24 00

Château Pontet-Canet
33250 Pauillac
05 56 59 04 04

Château Mouton Rothschild
33250 Pauillac
05 56 59 22 22

Château Pichon Longueville
33250 Pauillac
05 56 73 24 00

Château Pichon Longueville-
Comtesse de Lalande
33250 Pauillac
05 56 59 19 40

PÉCHARMANT

Château de Biran
24520 Saint-Sauveur-de-Bergerac
05 53 22 46 29

Château de Tiregand
24100 Creysse
05 53 23 21 08

Château La Tilleraie
24100 Pécharmant
05 53 57 86 42

Domaine du Haut-Pécharmant
24100 Bergerac
05 53 57 29 50

PESSAC-LÉOGNAN

BLANC
Domaine de Chevalier
33850 Léognan
05 56 64 16 16

Château La Garde
33650 Martillac
05 56 35 53 00

Château de Fieuzal
33580 Léognan
05 56 64 77 86

Château Smith Haut Lafitte
33650 Martillac
05 57 83 11 22

Château Larrivet-Haut-Brion
33850 Léognan
05 56 64 75 51

Château Couhins-Lurton
33420 Grézillac
05 57 25 58 58

Château Malartic-Lagravière
33850 Léognan
05 56 64 75 08

PESSAC-LÉOGNAN
ROUGE

Château de France
33850 Léognan
05 56 64 75 39

Château Haut-Bailly
33850 Léognan
05 56 64 75 11

Château Haut-Bergey
33850 Léognan
05 56 64 05 22

Château Haut-Brion
33602 Pessac
05 56 00 29 30

Château Malartic-Lagravière
33850 Léognan
05 56 64 75 08

Château La Louvière
33850 Léognan
05 57 25 58 58

Château Pape Clément
33600 Pessac
05 57 26 38 38

POMEROL
Château Clos du Clocher
33500 Pomerol
05 57 51 62 17

Château Croix de Gay
33500 Pomerol
05 57 51 19 05

Château la Conseillante
33500 Pomerol
05 57 51 15 32

Château l'Église-Clinet
33500 Pomerol
05 57 25 99 00

Château Lafleur
33240 Mouillac
05 57 84 44 03

Château Le Bon Pasteur
33500 Pomerol
05 57 51 10 94

Château Mazeyres
33501 Libourne
05 57 51 00 48

Château Petit-Village
33500 Pomerol
05 57 51 21 08

Château Trotanoy
33500 Pomerol
05 57 51 78 96

Vieux Château Certan
33500 Pomerol
05 57 51 17 33

POMMARD
Domaine Jean-Marc Boillot
21630 Pommard
03 80 22 71 29

Domaine de Courcel
21630 Pommard
03 80 22 10 64

Domaine Parent
21630 Pommard
03 80 22 15 08

Domaine Rebourgeon-Mure
21630 Pommard
03 80 22 75 39

Domaine Le Royer Girardin
21630 Pommard
03 80 22 59 69

POUILLY-FUMÉ
Château de Tracy
58150 Tracy-sur-Loire
03 86 26 15 12

Didier Dagueneau
58150 Saint-Andelain
03 86 39 15 62

Domaine des Berthiers Dagueneau
58150 Saint-Andelain
03 86 39 12 85

Domaine Redde
58150 Pouilly-sur-Loire
03 86 39 14 72

Maison Guy Saget
58150 Pouilly-sur-Loire
03 86 39 57 75

PULIGNY-MONTRACHET BLANC
Domaine du Château de Puligny
21190 Puligny-Montrachet
03 80 21 39 14

Domaine Leflaive
21190 Puligny-Montrachet
03 80 21 30 13

Domaine Louis Carillon
21190 Puligny-Montrachet
03 80 21 30 34

Domaine Sauzet
21190 Puligny-Montrachet
03 80 21 32 10

Maison Louis Jadot
21200 Beaune
03 80 22 10 57

QUINCY
Domaine Sallé
18120 Quincy
02 54 04 04 48

Domaine Sorbe
18120 Preuilly
02 48 51 99 43

Domaine du Tremblay
18120 Brinay
02 48 75 20 09

Domaine Trotereau
18120 Quincy
02 48 51 37 37

SAINT-ÉMILION
Château Angelus
33305 Saint-Émilion
05 57 24 71 39

Château Canon
33330 Saint-Émilion
05 57 55 23 45

Château Canon La Gaffelière
33330 Saint-Émilion
05 57 24 71 33

Château Chauvin
33330 Saint-Émilion
05 57 24 76 25

Château Cheval Blanc
33330 Saint-Émilion
05 57 55 55 55

Château Faugères
33330 Saint-Étienne-de-Lisse
05 57 40 34 99

Château Figeac
33330 Saint-Émilion
05 57 24 72 26

Château Larmande
33330 Saint-Émilion
05 57 24 71 41

Château Moulin Saint-Georges
33330 Saint-Émilion
05 57 24 70 26

Château Pavie
33330 Saint-Émilion
05 57 55 43 43

Château Troplong Mondot
33300 Saint-Émilion
05 57 55 32 05

Château La Couspaude
33330 Saint-Émilion
05 57 40 15 76

SAUTERNES

Château Gilette
33210 Preignac
05 56 76 28 44

Château Lafaurie-Peyraguey
33210 Bommes
05 57 19 57 77

Château Raymond-Lafon
33210 Sauternes
05 56 63 21 02

Château de Rayne Vigneau
33210 Bommes
05 56 11 29 00

Château Rieussec
33210 Fargues
05 57 98 14 14

Château d'Yquem
33210 Sauternes
05 56 63 21 02

SAVENNIÈRES

Château d'Épire
49170 Savennières
02 41 77 20 59

Coulée de Serrant
49170 Savennières
02 41 72 28 20

Domaine du Closel
49170 Savennières
02 41 72 81 00

Domaine Pierre Soulez
49170 Savennières
02 41 77 20 04

SAVIGNY-LÈS-BEAUNE ROUGE

Daniel Largeot
21200 Chorey-lès-Beaune
03 80 22 15 10

Domaine Chandon de Brialles
21420 Savigny-lès-Beaune
03 80 21 52 31

Domaine Rapet
21420 Pernand-Vergelesses
03 80 21 59 94

Domaine Simon Bize et Fils
21420 Savigny-lès-Beaune
03 80 21 50 57

TAVEL

Château de Trinquevedel
30126 Tavel
04 66 50 04 04

Domaine de la Mordorée
30126 Tavel
04 66 50 00 75

Domaine Roc de l'Olivet
30126 Tavel
04 66 50 37 87

Domaine Verda
30126 Tavel
04 66 82 87 28

TURSAN BLANC

Château de Bachen
40800 Duhort-Bachen
05 58 71 76 76

Château de Perchade
40320 Payros-Cazautets
05 58 44 50 68

Les Vignerons de Tursan
40320 Geaune
05 58 44 51 25

VIN DE SAVOIE CHIGNIN BERGERON

Domaine André et Michel Quénard
73800 Chignin
04 79 28 12 75

Domaine Raymond Quénard
73800 Chignin
04 79 28 01 46

Domaine Louis Magnin
73800 Arbin
04 79 84 12 12

VOSNE-ROMANÉE

Domaine Anne Gros
21700 Vosne-Romanée
03 80 61 05 95

Domaine des Perdrix
71640 Mercurey
03 85 98 12 12

Domaine Jayer Henri
21700 Vosne-Romanée
03 80 61 03 84

Domaine Leroy
21190 Auxey-Duresses
03 80 21 21 10

Domaine Méo-Camuzet
21700 Vosne-Romanée
03 80 61 11 05

Domaine Mongeard-Mugneret
21700 Vosne-Romanée
03 80 61 11 95

Maison Dominique Laurent
21700 Nuits-Saint-Georges
03 80 61 31 62

Maison Faiveley
21700 Nuits-Saint-Georges
03 80 61 04 55

ACKNOWLEDGMENTS

This book is the product of many years' meetings and experiences, getting to know the fabulous world of taste and flavour. I would like to thank all those people who guided me along the way, my own partners in flavour and friends: wine producers, fellow sommeliers, chefs, cellar-masters, journalists and wine lovers.

My thanks also to Anne Vantal and Blandine Houdart for their practical assistance.

Special thanks are due to photographer Jean-Charles Vaillant and food stylist Eric Trochon, for expressing in images what I wanted the flavours to say. Thanks too to all those people who made the photography possible, welcoming us onto their premises or lending us props. Special thanks to Harry and Marc, Isabelle and Jean-Luc, Anne and Pierre-Yves; also to Jaune de Chrome-Palais Royal and to Cristalleries Royales de Champagne. My thanks to the team at Bistrot du Sommelier, particularly my head chef Jean-André Lallican and my master sommelier and maître d'hôtel Xavier Guillien for their help with logistics.

Thank you Nadine, Célia and Mathias for being my partners in flavour on an everyday basis.

EDITORIAL DIRECTION

Blandine Houdart

CREATIVE DIRECTION

Nancy Dorking

DESIGN AND PRODUCTION

François Huertas

ORIGINATION

Penez Édition, Lille

PRINTING

Editoriale Lloyd en Italie

Dépôt Légal: 66775 - décembre 2005
ISBN : 2 851 20634 6
65. 4123. 9 - 01